W9-ATG-781

What's Black and White and Reid All Over?

Something Hilarious Happened at the Library

ROB REID

American Library Association
Chicago   2012

Rob Reid is the very popular author of numerous books on children's programming for ALA Editions. He has also written resources for Upstart Books and is the author of two picture books. In addition, he writes regular columns on programming and children's literature for *LibrarySparks* magazine and has a column in *Book Links* magazine titled "Reid-Aloud Alert." Rob is senior lecturer at the University of Wisconsin–Eau Claire and conducts workshops across North America on ways to make literature come alive for children. Rob can be contacted through www.rapnrob.com.

Printed in the United States of America
16 15 14 13 12   5 4 3 2 1

While extensive effort has gone into ensuring the reliability of the information in this book, the publisher makes no warranty, express or implied, with respect to the material contained herein.

ISBN: 978-0-8389-1147-1 (paper); 978-0-8389-9403-0 (PDF); 978-0-8389-9404-7 (ePub); 978-0-8389-9405-4 (Mobipocket); 978-0-8389-9406-1 (Kindle). For more information on digital formats, visit the ALA Store at alastore.ala.org and select eEditions.

Library of Congress Cataloging-in-Publication Data
Reid, Rob.
  What's black and white and Reid all over? : something hilarious happened at the library / Rob Reid.
      pages   cm
  Includes bibliographical references and index.
  ISBN 978-0-8389-1147-1
  1. Children's libraries—Activity programs—United States. 2. Storytelling—United States.
3. Wit and humor, Juvenile—Bibliography. I. Title.
  Z718.3.R465 2012
  027.62'51—dc23
                                                                    2011043233

4430

Book design in Soft Compound and Liberation Serif by Casey Bayer.

♾ This paper meets the requirements of ANSI/NISO Z39.48-1992 (Permanence of Paper).

Dedicated to Vicki and Steve Palmquist,
creators of the Children's Literature Network,
my webmasters and good friends

———————

And also to three authors who continually shared their stories and talents
with my students at the University of Wisconsin–Eau Claire and
have become good friends over the years:

Julie Bowe
David LaRochelle
Marsha Qualey

CONTENTS

ACKNOWLEDGMENTS

THANKS TO my editor Stephanie Zvirin, who asked me to write this book and after I said no waited patiently for me to come around to her way of thinking.

Thanks, once again, to Eloise.

I'd like to thank the students, family members, and staff from the following schools and libraries for helping me shape many of the ideas found in this book:

- Augusta Elementary School and Augusta Public Library, Augusta, Wisconsin
- Fall Creek Elementary School, Fall Creek, Wisconsin
- Flynn Elementary School, Eau Claire, Wisconsin
- Greenwood Elementary School, Greenwood, Wisconsin
- Rice Lake Public Library, Rice Lake, Wisconsin

Thanks to the Children's Services staff at the L. E. Phillips Memorial Public Library, Eau Claire, Wisconsin.

Finally, hugs and kisses to my wife, Jayne; my children, Alice, Julia, Laura, and Sam; my sons-in-law, Kirk and Steven; and my grandson, Parker.

INTRODUCTION

"**MY JOB** is to make kids laugh."

That's how I opened my introduction to *Something Funny Happened at the Library* (ALA Editions, 2003). All of these years have passed, and I still feel this is one of my missions in life. It is very satisfying for me to see children laugh because of something I said, sang, or read to them. Humor is how I connect kids with literature and imagination.

In *Something Funny Happened at the Library*, I wrote a "Tricks of the Trade" chapter. I feel the words I wrote there on how to share humor with children still work today. Briefly, these are

1. prepare your audience;
2. be expressive;
3. find your voice;
4. experiment;
5. create your own material;
6. pace yourself;
7. avoid inappropriate humor; and
8. have fun.

Although I go into greater detail for each "trick" in that book, for this companion volume, I incorporated these tricks within each story-program lesson plan. Each picture book highlighted in the program section comes with its own "Storytelling Tip." For example, I might provide an audience-participation idea or a suggestion on how to deliver a certain sentence, verbally or nonverbally.

There are ten humor story programs in this book—five aimed at the preschool crowd and five at the school-age (kindergarten through fourth grade) audience. With minor tweaking, a storyteller can use all ten programs for either of these audiences as well as an intergenerational or family story program.

Another difference between this book and its predecessor is the inclusion of the "Laugh-Out-Loud Selections" for many of the chapter books listed in part 3, "The Funniest Books in Your Library." These helpful additions are modeled after the "10 Minute Selection" feature in both my *Book Links* magazine column, "Reid-Aloud Alert," and my books *Reid's Read-Alouds* (ALA Editions, 2009) and *Reid's Read-Alouds 2* (ALA Editions, 2011). These stand-alone passages are designed for librarians and teachers to share quality literature time when there isn't an opportunity to read aloud the whole book.

"The Funniest Books in Your Library" section is grouped into the following categories: "Picture Books," "Easy Readers," "Graphic Novels/Manga" (a category new to this edition), "Chapter Books," "Poetry," and "Derivative Literature"—picture-book parodies of traditional folklore and songs. These lists feature books published between 2000 and 2010 (yes, I added another year to the decade). The target audiences for these books are preschool- through middle-school-age readers, with the understanding that many books of interest to upper-elementary-school-age readers are also of interest to middle-school-age readers. This aligns with the Newbery Award age-range criteria of target audience up to age fourteen. All books are in print and available for purchase from major vendors at the time of this writing. These titles are listed as a follow-up to those humor books featured in *Something Funny Happened at the Library*. Joke books are not listed because of space constraints.

The books featured in the programming sections and the "Funniest Books in Your Library" section have one thing in common—they are funny. Adults might not find some of them funny at all, but kids will. Some of the books feature very subtle aspects of humor, while others display laugh-out-loud, side-splitting, milk-comes-out-your-nose humor.

The programs and the books are kid-tested and ready for you to share. Enjoy.

HUMOR PROGRAMS FOR THE PRESCHOOL CROWD

1

"F" IS FOR FUNNY
(AND FUN)

ALL OF the books and activities in this program feature the letter *F*. Before reading each book, hold it up and ask the kids if they can figure out the *F* connection.

Program at a Glance

Opening Picture Book: *Pigs to the Rescue* by John Himmelman

Movement Activity: "Faster, Faster" by Rob Reid

Picture Book: *My Lucky Day* by Keiko Kasza

Picture Book: *Tiny Little Fly* by Michael Rosen and Kevin Waldron

Movement Activity: "Fee Fi Fo Fum" by Rob Reid

Picture Book: *Swim! Swim!* by James Proimos

Movement Activity: "Flip, Flop" by Rob Reid

Closing Picture Book: *Can You Make a Scary Face?* by Jan Thomas

Opening Picture Book

Himmelman, John. *Pigs to the Rescue.* Holt, 2010.

Farmer Greenstalk and his family have a variety of problems. The pigs on the farm yell, "Pigs to the rescue!" and help out. When the farmer's tractor breaks down, the pigs plow the field with everything from shovels to spoons. When Mrs. Greenstalk's garden hose has a leak, the pigs show up with containers of water, soaking not only the garden but Mrs. Greenstalk as well. After a series of similar events, a cat knocks over her saucer of milk. Everyone freezes. They really don't want the pigs to show up. "'That was close,' said Mrs. Greenstalk." The last illustration shows a herd of cows rushing toward the farmhouse with containers of milk.

Storytelling Tip: The kids will automatically join in every time the pigs yell, "Pigs to the rescue!" When the rooster has a sore throat and the pigs make noises to wake everyone, ask the children to squeal and oink as loudly as they can.

Movement Activity

"Faster, Faster" by Rob Reid.

The children can do this sitting down. Tell them you are going to give them directions, and when they hear the word *stop*, they must stop as fast as possible. As you recite the following, say each word slowly; then ask them to go faster. Let a few seconds go by, and then repeat the word *faster*! Let them continue at a very fast speed for about five more seconds before the "Stop!" command.

> Blink your eyes very slowly . . . now faster . . . faster! Stop!
> Wiggle your tongue very slowly . . . now faster . . . faster! Stop!
> Shrug your shoulders very slowly . . . now faster . . . faster! Stop!
> Clap your hands very slowly . . . now faster . . . faster! Stop!

After the clapping verse, I usually jokingly take a little bow and thank them for clapping.

Picture Book

Kasza, Keiko. *My Lucky Day*. Putnam, 2003.

A fox is surprised when a pig appears at his door. The pig seems to be surprised, too. The fox grabs the pig and a roasting pan. "This must be my lucky day. How often does dinner come knocking on the door?" The pig convinces the fox that he's too dirty to eat. The fox gives the pig a bath. Next, the pig suggests that he's too small to eat. The fox makes the pig a meal of spaghetti and cookies. The pig tells the fox that he's too tough to eat. The fox gives the pig a massage. Finally, the fox collapses from exhaustion. The pig runs away (with the rest of the cookies), looks at his address book (we see that the fox and a coyote have check marks next to their names), and wonders which animal he'll visit next. The last illustration shows the pig "accidentally" appearing at a bear's doorstep.

Storytelling Tip: Simply wink at the kids at the end of the story. They'll catch on that the pig knows what he's doing. This makes a good segue, because a series of winks is featured in the next picture book.

Picture Book

Rosen, Michael. *Tiny Little Fly*. Illustrated by Kevin Waldron. Candlewick, 2010.

A tiny little fly settles on an elephant's nose. The elephant winks and says, "I'm going to catch that fly!" The elephant winks its other eye, and the fly gets away. The same thing happens when the fly settles on a hippo's ear and a tiger's claws. This oversize book has foldout pages that show all three large animals making big noises while trying to catch the fly. In the end, the fly winks and says, "See you all soon. Bye, everyone, bye!"

Storytelling Tip: Before you begin reading the book, have a practice "winking session" with the kids. You'll see a variety of face-scrunching efforts as the kids give winking a try. Teach them the phrase, "I'm going to catch that fly," as it's repeated three times in the story. Take advantage of the loud noises the big animals make with your vocalization and gestures. The kids will giggle at your efforts.

Movement Activity

"Fee Fi Fo Fum" by Rob Reid.

Have the children stand. Inform them that some giants say, "Fee fi fo fum," and that they are going to act out a variety of animals, things, and people that start with the letter *F*.

> Fee fi fo fum,
> I'm not a giant,
> I'm a Frog! (*Kids act like frogs any way they want to express themselves. They usually say "Ribbit" and hop around.*)

> Fee fi fo fum,
> I'm not a giant,
> I'm a Fish! (*Kids pretend they are fish.*)

> Fee fi fo fum,
> I'm not a giant,
> I'm a Fly! (*Kids pretend they are flies.*)

> Fee fi fo fum,
> I'm not a giant,
> I'm a Forest! (*You may have to help them with this one. We usually stand closer together with hands over our heads, fingers splayed, as if we are trees in a forest.*)

> Fee fi fo fum,
> I'm not a giant,
> I'm a Friend! (*Tell the kids to give each other a high five.*)

Picture Book

Proimos, James. *Swim! Swim!* Scholastic, 2010.

Lerch, a pet fish, tells his story of looking for a friend. First, he spots some pebbles at the bottom of his tank and asks, "Pebbles, will you be my friend?" After getting no response, he spots a fishbowl deep-sea diver and asks, "Sir, would you be my friend?" The diver, of course, doesn't respond. Lerch starts crying after assuming the diver is rejecting him. "Good thing you can't see tears underwater." Next, Lerch hears bubbles and tries to talk to them. "I'll try talking bubble." A cat shows up outside Lerch's tank. The cat mistakes Lerch's name for "lunch." The cat moves Lerch to another tank, where Lerch meets Dinah, or as the cat says, "dinner." The two fish enjoy each other immensely.

Storytelling Tip: When Lerch tries to talk to the bubbles, he says, "Blub, blub, blub, blub," over and over. Ask the kids to join you in "bubble talk."

Movement Activity

"Flip, Flop" by Rob Reid.

Ask the children to stand and follow your instructions. I'd like to give a nod to Monty Python's Flying Circus and their "Ministry of Silly Walks" sketch for the inspiration of this idea.

> Flip, Flop
> Drip, Drop,
> Time to move
> So ever funny,
> Let me see you move *super slow*. (*Let the kids walk*
>   *around the room moving in slow motion.*)
>
> Flip, Flop,
> Drip, Drop,
> Time to move
> So ever funny,
> Let me see you move *teeny tiny*. (*Move with miniature*
>   *movements, such as tiny steps and tiny hand gestures.*)
>
> Flip, Flop,
> Drip, Drop,
> Time to move
> So ever funny,
> Let me see you move *backward*. (*Model moving*
>   *backward slowly, cautioning kids to keep an eye*
>   *on where they are going and to go slowly.*)

Flip, Flop,
Drip, Drop,
Time to move
So ever funny,
Let me see you (*pause*) *sit down*! (*Surprise them
    by sitting quickly. They'll follow.*)

Closing Picture Book

Thomas, Jan. *Can You Make a Scary Face?* Beach Lane, 2009.

This highly interactive picture book has a bug asking the kids in the audience to stand up, sit down, stand up again, wiggle a pretend bug off your nose, laugh, blow, do the chicken dance, and make a scary face when a big frog shows up. The bug is so frightened by the children's scary faces, he runs away with the frog.

Storytelling Tip: I wish there were more books like this. The text will do all the work for you. Just be sure to read at a nice, even pace, and don't rush.

Consider Substituting These Picture Books

There are many directions you can take with other *F* stories. Here are a few more:

Arnold, Tedd. *Frog in Space.* Dial, 2009.

Wilma the frog is minding her own business when a UFO lands in her swamp. An alien child who looks a lot like a blue frog slips out of its spacesuit and goes for a swim. Wilma is accidentally grabbed and thrown into the spaceship. The alien parents discover Wilma high up in outer space and decide the Earth water turned her green. When Wilma chases a fly, she hits the spaceship's controls, and the ship heads back to Earth. The aliens boot Wilma out the door and grab their child.

Storytelling Tip: Wilma is constantly chasing flies throughout the story. Ask the children to make buzzing sounds when they see her doing so.

Darbyshire, Kristen. *Put It on the List!* Dutton, 2009.

A family of chickens is constantly running out of food and other items. They have pancakes but no syrup; toothbrushes but no toothpaste ("Mom, chickens don't have teeth"); and cookies but no milk. Mom finally flips out and makes a meal out of whatever is in the house. This results in "peanut butter and pickled grub on macaroni casserole." The new family policy becomes—make a list!

Storytelling Tip: After reading the book, produce your own checklist and look it over, saying to yourself (loud enough for the children to hear), "Hmmm . . . let's see. Picture books . . . check. Story room . . . check. Storyteller . . . check. Kids? Where are the kids?" Of course, the kids will all yell, "HERE!"

Harrison, Joanna. *Grizzly Dad.* David Fickling, 2008.

A boy notices that his father wakes up in a terrible mood. "He grrroaned and grrrizzled . . . and GRRRUMPED!" The father goes back to sleep. When the boy tries to wake him up, we learn that Dad has turned into a grizzly bear. The two have fun at the park and in a movie theater. All of the other movie patrons are too frightened to enter. Back at home, the bear gives the boy a great big bear hug and turns back into Dad.

Storytelling Tip: Pause after reading the first double-page spread, about Dad waking up in a "GRRRRIZZLY" mood. Point out that two kids are fighting on top of Dad, one is sticking his finger up Dad's nose, the cat is scratching itself on Dad's head, and the dog is taking off with Dad's glasses. Ask your audience, "Wouldn't you be in a GRRRRIZZLY mood, too?"

Plourde, Lynn. *Field Trip Day.* Illustrated by Thor Wickstrom. Dutton, 2010.

Mrs. Shepherd's class goes on a field trip to Farmer Fandangle's Organic, Environmentally Friendly Farm. The first stop is to see the cows. One student goes missing. It's Juan. They find him and move on to the chickens. Once again, Juan goes missing. He shows up checking out the wind turbines. This continues until the farmer realizes two of his calves—earmarked to be sent to a charity—are missing. It's Juan who finds them—on the farmer's bed. "I just thought about where I'd wander off to if I was leaving home for the first time . . . Someplace cozy."

Storytelling Tip: Every time the teachers take a head count, lead the audience members in counting along.

Willems, Mo. *Today I Will Fly!* Hyperion, 2007.

Friends Elephant and Piggie are hanging out when Piggie decides that she wants to fly. A dog chases Piggie, and she goes up into the air, convinced she flew. Elephant points out that she jumped. A pelican comes along and helps Piggie fly with a rope. Elephant is excited for his friend.

Storytelling Tip: Play up Piggie's last line in the book. Elephant states, "Tomorrow I will fly!" Piggie looks at the reader. Take the time to look out at the audience with a look of disbelief. Piggie puts her hoof by her mouth and says, "Good luck." Say this phrase out of the side of your mouth.

2

MOO HA-HA

Program at a Glance

Opening Joke: "Knock-Knock Joke #2" from *Amazing Cows* by Sandra Boynton

Picture Book: *A Birthday for Cow!* by Jan Thomas

Picture Book/Puppet/Prop: *Fair Cow* by Leslie Helakoski

Call-and-Response Chant: "Day One at Cow Camp"
from *Amazing Cows* by Sandra Boynton

Short Story: "Cow Story" from *Amazing Cows* by Sandra Boynton

Fingerplay: "A Cow Has a Horn" by Rob Reid

Picture Book: *Everywhere the Cow Says "Moo!"* by Ellen
Slusky Weinstein and Kenneth Andersson

Musical Activity: "10 in the Field," traditional, with new words by Rob Reid

Closing Picture Book/Puppet/Prop: *Kiss the Cow*
by Phyllis Root and Will Hillenbrand

Opening Joke

**Boynton, Sandra. "Knock-Knock Joke #2,"
from *Amazing Cows*. Workman, 2010.**

Start off this silly program with an old joke found in a new book. A chicken and a cow are sharing a knock-knock joke. The chicken, standing by a nest of eggs, says, "Knock-knock." The cow says, "Who's there?" The chicken says, "Hatch." The cow says, "Hatch who?" The eggs hatch, and the newly born chicks yell, "Gesundheit!"

Storytelling Tip: Display the page so your audience can see the characters, or instruct the kids to say the cow's lines as you read the joke aloud.

Picture Book

Thomas, Jan. *A Birthday for Cow!* Harcourt, 2008.

Pig and Mouse are making a cake for Cow's birthday. Duck wants to help by adding a turnip to the cake. Next, Duck suggests they mix the batter with a turnip instead of a spoon. Duck wants to stick a turnip in the oven with the cake and top the cake with a turnip instead of candles. Pig and Mouse are not happy with the turnip. When Cow arrives, she is excited to see . . . the turnip.

Storytelling Tip: If possible, bring in a turnip as a prop simply to display during the story. The children can look at it and wonder what its appeal is for duck and cow.

Picture Book/Puppet/Prop

**Helakoski, Leslie. *Fair Cow*.
Marshall Cavendish, 2010.**

Effie the cow wants to be a state-fair prizewinning cow. "She dreamed of being beautiful, of billowing blue ribbons and big, bodacious barns." Petunia the pig, the 2000 Pork Queen, convinces Effie she needs "to get gussied up a bit." They both exercise. Petunia curls Effie's hair, dyes her spots, paints her hooves, adds a tail extension, and modifies her walk. When Effie sees how beautiful the other cow contestants are, she feels sick "to all four parts of her stomach." She gets messy as the day progresses but still wins a prize—for Best Milk.

Storytelling Tip: Use a cow puppet or plush toy to represent Effie. There are several on the market. Pretend the puppet is exercising during this part of the story by moving it up and down as if it's jogging. Twist it side to side as if it is "jazzercising." Add hair curlers to its head and a felt or fuzzy "hair extension" to its tail, or as close to the puppet's bottom as you can get. Mime painting dye and nail polish on its spots and hooves. Because a hand puppet might not have hooves, pretend they are there. You can also exaggerate twisting the puppet around as if it was walking and swaying like a supermodel. Attach a homemade blue ribbon with the words "Best Milk" to the cow at the end of the story.

Call-and-Response Chant

**"Day One at Cow Camp" from *Amazing Cows*
by Sandra Boynton.**

Read the kids both parts of the cow-camp chant from Boynton's book. Then repeat. You read the leader's part, and your audience will know what is expected from them. Start with "Do you want to be a cow?" The audience responds with "Yes, we want to be a cow!" There are parts where everyone goes "mooooo" as well as making quacking noises. When you, the leader, apologize for that little quacking mishap, the kids repeat the apology. Feel free to embellish the chant with your own additional comments.

Short Story

**"Cow Story" from *Amazing Cows*
by Sandra Boynton.**

"Once upon a time, there were 137 cows that lived very happily on a lovely farm in North Dakota or something." The narrator proceeds to name the cows. After reading several names, including Milo, Debit, Big George, and Steve, the narrator concludes the litany with "The remaining eighty cows were all named Tino, which was not a good idea." The cows play the traditional game Red Rover, Red Rover with some chickens. As the game progresses, one of the chickens ignorantly shouts, "Red Rover, Red Rover, let Tino come over!" Of course, the eighty cows named Tino charge the line.

Storytelling Tip: Before the chicken tells the Tinos to come over, other players yell for "Walter" and then "Trixie" to come over. Tell your audience these names and have them join you in the traditional "Red Rover, Red Rover" chant.

Fingerplay

"A Cow Has a Horn" by Rob Reid.

A cow has a horn here (*Hold up your right hand,*
 with the forefinger in the air.)
And she has a horn there (*Hold up your pinkie finger. You'll*
 need to hold down the two middle fingers with your thumb.
 The end result will look like two horns on a cow's head.)
In between some fur. (*Run a finger from your left hand over the*
 knuckles of your two middle fingers as if petting fur.)
You need to be careful (*Shake the forefinger of*
 your left hand as if warning someone.)
She doesn't poke you (*Point the "horns"—the forefinger and pinkie on*
 the right hand—sideways, as if jabbing someone with the horns.)
When you go to milk her. (*Turn your right hand so the*
 "horns" point downward and become "udders." Grab the
 "udders" with your left hand as if milking the cow.)

Picture Book

Weinstein, Ellen Slusky. *Everywhere the Cow Says "Moo!"*
Illustrated by Kenneth Andersson. Boyds Mills, 2008.

The sounds of the dog, the frog, the duck, and the rooster are given in English, Spanish, French, and Japanese. After each of the animals above is featured, we learn that "everywhere the cow says 'Moo!'"

Storytelling Tip: It's fun to see a young audience's quizzical looks when they hear that in some parts of the world, a dog may bark "Goo-ow" or "Wan-wan." Or that a frog might croak "Crew-ah" or "Kero kero." The children will automatically chime in with the cow's "Moo," including the extra-long one at the end of the book.

Musical Activity

"10 in the Field," traditional, with new words by Rob Reid.

Tell the children to hold up ten fingers. Each finger represents a cow that needs to leave the field to go into the barn. The children should lower one finger with each verse until there are no fingers in the air. You'll find the children will also enjoy shouting, "Moo-ve over!" with emphasis on the "Moo" part.

Sing to the tune of the traditional song "10 in the Bed."

>There were 10 in the field, and the farmer called out,
>"Moo-ve over!"
>So they all moved over, and one went in the barn.
>
>There were 9 in the field, and the farmer called out,
>"Moo-ve over!"
>So they all moved over, and one went in the barn.
>
>There were 8 in the field, and the farmer called out,
>"Moo-ve over!"
>So they all moved over, and one went in the barn.
>
>There were 7 in the field, and the farmer called out,
>"Moo-ve over!"
>So they all moved over, and one went in the barn.
>
>There were 6 in the field, and the farmer called out,
>"Moo-ve over!"
>So they all moved over, and one went in the barn.
>
>There were 5 in the field, and the farmer called out,
>"Moo-ve over!"
>So they all moved over, and one went in the barn.
>
>There were 4 in the field, and the farmer called out,
>"Moo-ve over!"
>So they all moved over, and one went in the barn.
>
>There were 3 in the field, and the farmer called out,
>"Moo-ve over!"
>So they all moved over, and one went in the barn.
>
>There were 2 in the field, and the farmer called out,
>"Moo-ve over!"
>So they all moved over, and one went in the barn.

There was 1 in the field, and the farmer called out,
"Moo-ve over!"
So the cow moved over, and she went in the barn.

There were none left in the field, and the farmer called out,
"Moo-vie time!"

Closing Picture Book/Puppet/Prop

Root, Phyllis. *Kiss the Cow*. Illustrated by Will Hillenbrand. Candlewick, 2000.

Mama May milks her magic cow, Luella, every day to feed her many children. She sings a little chant: "Lovely Luella / Your milk never fails / My children are hungry / So please fill my pails." After Luella gives her milk, Mama May says, "Thank you, Luella / My children shall eat / Cheese fresh and yellow / Milk warm and sweet." Mama May then kisses Luella on the nose. Annalisa, the youngest of Mama May's brood, thinks kissing a cow is disgusting. The little one decides to milk Luella herself. She says the proper words but doesn't give a kiss at the end. Luella refuses to give milk after that, and "Mama May's house was full of hungry, crying children." At first, Annalisa stubbornly resists kissing the cow, but she finally does.

Storytelling Tip: Teach the children Mama May's two short chants before you read the picture book. They can join you in saying them at the appropriate times during the story. At the end of the book, bring out the cow puppet or plush toy and allow all children who want to kiss it on the nose to do so as they file out of the story area.

Consider Substituting These Picture Books

Allen, Jonathan. *The Little Rabbit Who Liked to Say Moo*. Boxer, 2008.

A little rabbit enjoys saying "Moo." He also likes to say "Baaa," "Oink Oink Oink," "Hee Haw," and "Quack." Of course, he is joined by a calf, a lamb, a piglet, a baby donkey, and a duckling. They all agree that the noise they each make is the noise they enjoy the most. Little Rabbit begs to differ. The rabbit finishes the book by saying "Woof!"

Storytelling Tip: This will be a fun sound-effects book for the audience to chime in with the animals.

Duffield, Katy S. *Farmer McPeepers and His Missing Milk Cows*. Illustrated by Steve Gray. Rising Moon, 2003.

Nearsighted Farmer McPeepers loses his glasses (the cows took them). He goes looking for them. He passes by some fishermen on Meyer's Pond (your audience will laugh to see the fishermen are cows), youngsters swimming (more cows), children playing on the town's playground (cows), and so on. Farmer McPeepers stumbles across his glasses and, once he puts them on, is surprised to find himself surrounded by his cows.

Storytelling Tip: As you read the picture book, give an occasional, exaggerated squint as Farmer McPeepers is looking around without his glasses.

Fox, Mem. *A Particular Cow*. Illustrated by Terry Denton. Harcourt, 2006.

A cow goes on her Saturday morning walk and "finds herself on the wrong side of a particular pair of bloomers." They cover up her eyes, and she runs into a particular woman, a particular postman, three particular dogs, a particular party of children, a particular bridegroom and bride (knocking the bride into a lake), and a particular gang of sailors. She rights herself and goes "on her way without surprise, on that particular Saturday morning."

Storytelling Tip: Be sure to read the many word balloons that the cow and the other characters say. The particular woman calls the cow a "bloomin' thief," because the cow stumbled into a clothesline and is wearing the woman's bloomers on her head.

French, Jackie. *Too Many Pears!* Illustrated by Bruce Whatley. Star Bright, 2003.

Pamela the cow loves pears. She likes them fresh, she likes them stewed, and she likes them in a pie. Her owners build a fence around the pear tree, but Pamela "crawl[s] through a wombat hole under the fence." They tie her to a tree, but she uproots the tree in her quest for pears. The little girl Amy decides to feed Pamela as many pears as possible. "Pamela ate 600 pears. And then she stopped. Pamela wasn't smiling anymore." Pamela starts eating apples.

Storytelling Tip: After hearing how many ways Pamela eats pears, ask your audience if they can think of unusual ways to prepare and eat pears. Possible responses from this brief brainstorming session might include pear pancakes, pear chili, pizza with pepperoni and pears, and pear shakes.

Harris, Trudy, and Jay Harris. *Wow, It's a Cow*. Illustrated by Paige Keiser. Scholastic, 2010.

This lift-the-flap book has a farmer looking for his cow. He thinks he sees the cow pulling a plow, but when the flap is raised, we see a horse. The farmer next thinks he sees the cow in the mud. Of course, the raised flap reveals a pig. This pattern continues with a duck in a pond, a sheep in a field, and a bird in a tree. We finally catch up to the cow when we open the barn doors.

Storytelling Tip: The kids will enjoy guessing what's behind each flap. Pause in between each "revealing" to let them shout out their guesses.

Wilson, Karma. *The Cow Loves Cookies.*
Illustrated by Marcellus Hall. Margaret K. McElderry, 2010.

The horse loves hay, the chickens eat chicken feed, the geese have cracked corn, the pigs enjoy slop, the dog receives doggie treats, and the cow loves cookies. Why does the cow love cookies? The farmer and the cow worked out a deal. The farmer takes cookies from a tin, and the cow provides the milk "to dunk them in."

Storytelling Tip: Make felt images of the horse, a few chickens, a few geese, a pig, a dog, a cow, the farmer, a bale of hay, a bag of chicken feed, a bag of cracked corn, a bucket of slop, a doggie treat, and a cookie. Place them on the felt board as they appear in the story. Point to the animals as they reappear in the story so the children can state what they are and what they eat. Felt patterns can be found on several Internet sites, or you can model your patterns from the images in the picture book.

3

NAUGHTY OR NICE

Program at a Glance

Opening Picture Book: *Hattie the Bad* by Jane Devlin and Joe Berger

Song: "I Know a Song That Gets on Everybody's Nerves," traditional

Picture Book: *Froggy Eats Out* by Jonathan London and Frank Remkiewicz

Movement Activity: "No, No, No, No, Yes, Yes, Yes" by Rob Reid

Picture Book: *Ivan the Terrier* by Peter Catalanotto

Movement Activity: "The Grand Old Storyteller," traditional, with new words by Rob Reid

Picture Book/Fingerplay: *Ten Naughty Little Monkeys* by Suzanne Williams and Suzanne Watts

Picture Book: *Have You Been Naughty or Nice?* by Ethan Long

Closing Musical Activity: "Little Bunny Foo Foo," traditional

Opening Picture Book

Devlin, Jane. *Hattie the Bad*. Illustrated by Joe Berger. Dial, 2010.

Hattie puts frogs in her parents' refrigerator and ties her daddy's car keys to helium-filled balloons. Her parents claim she was dropped on her head as a baby. Hattie eventually decides to be good. She becomes the perfect child. As she is about to accept the award for "The Best-Behaved Child Ever," Hattie reverts to her old self and yells, "Underpants" during her acceptance speech. "Hattie the Bad was back (with just a teensy bit of good)."

Storytelling Tip: Follow the various font changes to know which words to emphasize. Take advantage of the bold "Bad" and the scripted "Good," and exaggerate these two words when you read them.

Song

"I Know a Song That Gets on Everybody's Nerves," traditional.

Sing this old camp song to the tune of "John Brown's Body." Sing it a few times with the kids, and then do a mock scream and cover your ears.

> I know a song that gets on everybody's nerves,
> I know a song that gets on everybody's nerves,
> I know a song that gets on everybody's nerves
> And this is how it goes . . . (*Repeat.*)

Picture Book

London, Jonathan. *Froggy Eats Out*. Illustrated by Frank Remkiewicz. Viking, 2001.

Froggy and his parents go to a fancy restaurant called Chez Yum. He knocks over a glass of water, hits the waiter with a spoon, hops loudly around the restaurant, and pulls the tablecloth off—and everything on it. The family decides to leapfrog over to Speedy's diner, where they eat "burgers and flies."

Storytelling Tip: As with all of London's Froggy books, there are a lot of sound effects written into the text. For example, as Froggy gets dressed, he buttons his shirt—"zut! zut! zut!"—and ties his shoes—"zwit! zwit!" Exaggerate these words and mime most of them, too. The children in the audience will instinctively follow suit.

Movement Activity

"No, No, No, No, Yes, Yes, Yes" by Rob Reid.

Have the children shake their heads "no" and nod "yes" at the appropriate times during this chant.

> Should I kick the cat? Should I kick the cat?
> No! No! No! No!
> Should I pet the cat? Should I pet the cat?
> Yes! Yes! Yes!
>
> Shall I spit my food? Shall I spit my food?
> No! No! No! No!
> Shall I swallow my food? Shall I swallow my food?
> Yes! Yes! Yes!
>
> Shall I write on the walls? Shall I write on the walls?
> No! No! No! No!
> Shall I write on paper? Shall I write on paper?
> Yes! Yes! Yes!
>
> Shall I push my parents? Shall I push my parents?
> No! No! No! No!
> Shall I hug my parents? Shall I hug my parents?
> Yes! Yes! Yes!

Picture Book

Catalanotto, Peter. *Ivan the Terrier.* Atheneum, 2007.

A terrier interjects himself into several traditional folktales and barks wildly at the characters. Children will recognize the Billy Goats Gruff, the Three Bears, the Three Pigs, and the Gingerbread Boy. The narrator constantly scolds Ivan, to no avail. Finally, the narrator starts reading a story starring Ivan. Ivan goes right to sleep.

Storytelling Tip: Have the children in the audience bark wildly with Ivan. They will bark first and then burst into giggles.

Movement Activity

"The Grand Old Storyteller," traditional, with new words by Rob Reid.

Have the children stand, make noise, jump, and sit during the appropriate lines in this updated version of the nursery rhyme "The Grand Old Duke of York."

> The Grand Old Storyteller,
> Has many girls and boys.
> Some are very good,
> Some make LOTS of noise.
> When they are bad, they jump,
> When they are good, they sit.
> But sometimes it's good to jump,
> Then sit, then jump, then sit (*pause*) again (*pause*) for the next story . . .

Picture Book/Fingerplay

**Williams, Suzanne. *Ten Naughty Little Monkeys.*
Illustrated by Suzanne Watts. HarperCollins, 2007.**

Author Williams wrote new verses for the traditional fingerplay "Ten Little Monkeys Jumping on the Bed." Her monkeys trip and land on the floor, slip and plop in their seat, skin their knees, hit a bump rolling down a hill, bend their tails, fall into water, tip over in a barrel, stub their toes, fall into a trap, and go back to jumping on the bed again.

Storytelling Tip: It's fairly easy to create new fingerplay motions for the new verses. For example, for "Seven little monkeys climbing up a tree," make climbing motions. For "One tumbled out and skinned his knee," swirl both hands around each other and then rub a knee. Feel free to be creative with the new verses. Don't hesitate to ask the children how *they* think the motions should be done.

Picture Book

Long, Ethan. *Have You Been Naughty or Nice?* Little, Brown, 2009.

Duck states that he has been a nice duck. He is bringing a plate of cookies for Santa Claus. The cookies smell delicious, and Duck eats them. He then worries that he's a naughty duck. He writes an apology, which appears in a lift-the-flap format. On the last double-page spread, we see a sleeping Duck surrounded by his presents and two departing boots in the fireplace.

Storytelling Tip: Make enormous gobbling noises and motions when Duck eats the cookies. Play up his shock when he realizes what he has done. Hold the last picture up a beat longer than usual to see if the children spot the subtle image of Santa's boots in the fireplace.

Closing Musical Activity

"Little Bunny Foo Foo," traditional.

Finish the program by telling the children they are going to sing about a naughty bunny rabbit named Foo Foo. Many will know this popular song. Teach them the motions that go with the song. The tune can be found on various sites on the Internet. Paul Brett Johnson has a picture-book version, *Little Bunny Foo Foo* (Scholastic, 2004), for those who would prefer using a book. The picture book contains a musical score in the back matter.

> Little Bunny Foo Foo (*Hold up two fingers to represent the bunny's ears.*)
> hoppin' through the forest, (*Move the two fingers up and down.*)
> scoopin' up the field mice (*Make a grabbing motion with one hand.*)
> and boppin' 'em on the head. (*Hit that hand with your other hand.*)
> Down came the Blue Fairy, (*Wiggle fingers in a downward motion.*)
> and she said:
> "Little Bunny Foo Foo (*Point finger as if scolding.*)
> I don't want to see you
> scoopin' up the field mice (*Make the grabbing motion again.*)
> and boppin' 'em on the head. (*Make the hitting motion again.*)
> And now I'll give you three chances, (*Hold up three fingers.*)
> and if you keep it up,
> I'll turn you into a goon." (*Make a scary face.*)
>
> Little Bunny Foo Foo (*Hold up two fingers to represent the bunny's ears.*)
> hoppin' through the forest, (*Move the two fingers up and down.*)
> scoopin' up the field mice (*Make a grabbing motion with one hand.*)
> and boppin' 'em on the head. (*Hit that hand with your other hand.*)
> Down came the Blue Fairy, (*Wiggle fingers in a downward motion.*)
> and she said:

"Little Bunny Foo Foo (*Point finger as if scolding.*)
I don't want to see you
scoopin' up the field mice (*Make the grabbing motion again.*)
and boppin' 'em on the head. (*Make the hitting motion again.*)
And now I'll give you two more chances, (*Hold up two fingers.*)
and if you keep it up,
I'll turn you into a goon." (*Make a scary face.*)

Little Bunny Foo Foo (*Hold up two fingers to represent the bunny's ears.*)
hoppin' through the forest, (*Move the two fingers up and down.*)
scoopin' up the field mice (*Make a grabbing motion with one hand.*)
and boppin' 'em on the head. (*Hit that hand with your other hand.*)
Down came the Blue Fairy, (*Wiggle fingers in a downward motion.*)
and she said:
"Little Bunny Foo Foo (*Point finger as if scolding.*)
I don't want to see you
scoopin' up the field mice (*Make the grabbing motion again.*)
and boppin' 'em on the head. (*Make the hitting motion again.*)
And now I'll give you one more chance, (*Hold up one finger.*)
and if you do it again,
I'll turn you into a goon." (*Make a scary face.*)

Little Bunny Foo Foo (*Hold up two fingers to represent the bunny's ears.*)
hoppin' through the forest, (*Move the two fingers up and down.*)
scoopin' up the field mice (*Make a grabbing motion with one hand.*)
and boppin' 'em on the head. (*Hit that hand with your other hand.*)
Down came the Blue Fairy, (*Wiggle fingers in a downward motion.*)
and she said:
"Little Bunny Foo Foo (*Point finger as if scolding.*)
I don't want to see you
scoopin' up the field mice (*Make the grabbing motion again.*)
and boppin' 'em on the head. (*Make the hitting motion again.*)
You disobeyed me three times, (*Hold up three fingers.*)
so now I'm gonna turn you into a GOON!" (*Make a scary face.*)
The moral of this story:
Hare today, GOON tomorrow!

Consider Substituting These Picture Books

Burningham, John. *Edwardo: The Horriblest Boy in the Whole Wide World.* Knopf, 2006.

Edwardo is scolded by adults for being rough, noisy, nasty, cruel, messy, and dirty. The more he hears these words, the worse he becomes. One day, an adult says a kind thing about him. And another and another. He eventually becomes "the nicest boy in the whole wide world."

Storytelling Tip: As each adult scolds Edwardo, wag your finger as if you were scolding him, too.

Demas, Corinne. *Always in Trouble.* Illustrated by Noah Z. Jones. Scholastic, 2004.

Toby the dog is in trouble every day. For example, every Monday, he gets into the garbage. His owner, Emma, takes him to dog-training school. He is the perfect student. However, once back home, he causes trouble again. He goes back to school to become "a specially trained dog." When he returns home this time, he takes out the garbage on Monday. He is *almost* a perfect dog.

Storytelling Tip: There is a torn hole in the last page of the book. It appears Toby caused it. Do a double-take when you hold up this page for your audience.

Lloyd-Jones, Sally. *Being a Pig Is Nice: A Child's-Eye View of Manners.* Illustrated by Dan Krall. Schwartz and Wade, 2009.

Sally imagines that if she were a pig, a snail, an elephant, a monkey, and an owl, she would have an excuse for not being clean, dawdling, splashing in the tub, eating with her fingers, or staying up late. However, with each animal comes a drawback. Pigs smell, snails are slimy, elephants have flies, monkeys have grubs in their ears, and owls throw up their breakfast. Sally settles for being a monster.

Storytelling Tip: After you read the story, ask the children if they can think of other animals. What would be an advantage to being that animal? What would be a drawback?

Rosoff, Meg. *Wild Boars Cook.* Illustrated by Sophie Blackall. Holt, 2008.

Four wild boars are "bossy and selfish and stinky and HUNGRY." They find a recipe to make a Massive Pudding. It includes ten cups of sugar, five hundred chocolate-covered chocolates, a gross of donuts, a bucket of butter, twenty-six bananas, and a squid. They eat their Massive Pudding "in ten seconds flat." They are satisfied . . . for five minutes before they are hungry again.

Storytelling Tip: When the boars dive into their Massive Pudding, ask the children to imitate the boars by making snorting noises.

Shannon, David. *David Gets in Trouble.* Scholastic, 2002.

David insists it's not his fault when he gets into trouble. He knocks over furniture while skateboarding indoors. He breaks a window with the baseball. He makes a silly face for the class picture. In the end, he apologizes.

Storytelling Tip: This book is a quick read. Slow it down by letting the children take a good look at each double-page spread before flipping the page.

Warburton, Tom. *1000 Times No.* HarperCollins, 2009.

Little Noah refuses to go when his mother tells him "it's time to leave." He not only says "No" but he says, "No way, Jose," "Nyet," "O-nay," and several other versions of the word *no*. When he learns that their destination is the playground, he lets out a loud "YES!"

Storytelling Tip: This requires a fair amount of setup, but this is a fun book to read with several coworkers. Each person can learn some of the various ways to say "No." There is a pronunciation guide for the foreign words. Some versions of "No" require visuals, such as a tattoo of the word or a vanity license plate. These could be reproduced pictures held up by the various storytellers. There is one double-page spread where a large crowd says, "Nooooooo!" Ask everyone in the room to loudly belt it out.

4

NOW I KNOW MY ABCs

Program at a Glance

Opening Song: "The Alphabet Song," traditional

Picture Book: *Bad Kitty* by Nick Bruel

Picture Book: *A Isn't for Fox: An Isn't Alphabet* by Wendy Ulmer and Laura Knorr

Movement Activity: "Letter Shape-xercise," traditional

Picture Book: *The Dog from Arf! Arf! to Zzzzzz* by the Dog Artlist Collection

Musical Activity: "Old MacDonald ABC," traditional, with new words by Rob Reid

Picture Book: *Alphabet* by Matthew Van Fleet

Closing Activity: Library Alphabet Scavenger Hunt

Opening Song

"The Alphabet Song," traditional.

Sing the well-known alphabet song in a variety of funny ways. Start off by asking the children if they know it. Have everyone sing it normally. Repeat it, but this time, sing it very fast. The kids will be guaranteed to giggle. Sing it a third time in a superslow manner. Sing it a fourth time in a high falsetto. Sing it next like a cat, meowing the whole time. Ask the children to sing it again in a whisper. Ask them to sing it one last time, only quieter than before. Next, mime singing the words. At the end, ask everyone to give themselves loud applause for such wonderful singing.

Picture Book

Bruel, Nick. *Bad Kitty.* Roaring Brook, 2005.

This inventive picture book goes through the alphabet not once, but four times. The first time around, Kitty is given a choice of fruits and vegetables to eat. Kitty performs an alphabetical litany of naughty things in retaliation. The third time through the alphabet, we see an odd assortment of weird food items. Apparently, Kitty likes these choices because she performs a series of good tasks for the fourth trip through the alphabet.

Storytelling Tip: Be sure to read the various notes that Kitty writes. Feel free to play up your vocals throughout the weirdness of the book. It will help keep the attention of the very young children. Have special fun drawing out the lines, "a very, very, bad, bad, BAD kitty."

Picture Book

Ulmer, Wendy. *A Isn't for Fox: An Isn't Alphabet.*
Illustrated by Laura Knorr. Sleeping Bear Press, 2008.

The premise for this alphabet book is that a few objects that *don't* start with the featured letter are prominent in the verse. There are, however, clues to the object that *does* begin with the letter. For example, "A isn't for box; it isn't for fox. A is for ants that crawl over your socks." We see a large fox with an oddly placed box. Many ants are crawling over the fox's socks.

Storytelling Tip: Before revealing which object pertains to each letter, pause and let the audience guess the correct word. Some illustrations are very helpful, and the objects are fairly clear to preschoolers. *B* has some bats prominently displayed. *C* has a cat sitting on a child's lap. Other objects will be difficult for anyone, let alone preschoolers. *N* is for nuthatch, and *X* is for Xenops, a tropical bird. That's OK. Just tell children that even grown-ups have trouble with those.

Movement Activity

"Letter Shape-xercise," traditional.

Because many alphabet books take a long time to plow through—especially for the preschool crowd—it's good to include a lot of movement breaks throughout the story program. "Letter Shape-xercise" is a term I came up with, although the idea of forming the human body into letters has been around for a long time. We did it in college theater classes. Ask the children to stand up and form the letter *A* with their bodies, arms, and legs. Model it for them. Spread your feet apart and join both hands overhead. It doesn't have to be an exact replica of the letter. Go through the entire alphabet. Ask them from time to time how *they* think the letters should be made.

Picture Book

The Dog Artlist Collection. *The Dog from Arf! Arf! to Zzzzzz.* HarperCollins, 2004.

This photographic and alphabetical portrayal of dogs is tailor-made for sound effects and movement activities. The first dog goes "Arf! Arf!" The second dog begs. The next dog follows the command "Come!" Each letter of the alphabet has a similar dog-related activity or sound effect.

Storytelling Tip: Have the children act like the dog portrayed as you show them each picture. Some favorites include "Howwwwl"; the dog that itches; "wag, wag, wag" (kids can wiggle their butts); and, of course, roll over. Some movements are similar to each other. Down and lie down will find the children doing the same motions. That's OK. They'll still have fun pretending to be dogs.

Musical Activity

"Old MacDonald ABC," traditional, with new words by Rob Reid.

Sing this to the tune of "Old MacDonald." Have the children stand and perform the actions or sound effects (or both) for each animal.

> Old MacDonald had a farm, E-I-E-I-O,
> And on her farm she had an Alligator, E-I-E-I-O,
> With a Snap-Snap here and a Snap-Snap there, (*Hold
> arms straight out and clap hands.*)

Here a Snap, there a Snap,
Everywhere a Snap-Snap,
Old MacDonald had a farm, E-I-E-I-O.

And on her farm she had a Badger, E-I-E-I-O,
With a Dig-Dig here and a Dig-Dig there, (*Mime
    a digging motion with hands.*)
Here a Dig, there a Dig,
Everywhere a Dig-Dig,
Old MacDonald had a farm, E-I-E-I-O.

And on her farm she had a Crab, E-I-E-I-O,
With a Click-Clack here and a Click-Clack there, (*Form
    claws with hands. Open and shut the thumb.*)
Here a Click, there a Clack,
Everywhere a Click-Clack,
Old MacDonald had a farm, E-I-E-I-O.

And on her farm she had a Dolphin, E-I-E-I-O,
With an Eee-Eee here and an Eee-Eee there, (*Hold head up as
    if sticking it out of the water while making the sound.*)
Here an Eee, there an Eee,
Everywhere an Eee-Eee,
Old MacDonald had a farm, E-I-E-I-O.

And on her farm she had an Elephant, E-I-E-I-O,
With a Trumpet noise here and a Trumpet noise
    there, (*Hold arm in front of nose.*)
Here a Trumpet, there a Trumpet,
Everywhere a Trumpet noise,
Old MacDonald had a farm, E-I-E-I-O.

And on her farm she had a Frog, E-I-E-I-O,
With a Croak-Croak here and a Croak-Croak there,
    (*Puff cheeks while making the sound.*)
Here a Croak, there a Croak,
Everywhere a Croak-Croak,
Old MacDonald had a farm, E-I-E-I-O.

And on her farm she had a Gorilla, E-I-E-I-O,
With a Thump-Thump here and a Thump-Thump
   there, (*Beat chest with hands.*)
Here a Thump, there a Thump,
Everywhere a Thump-Thump,
Old MacDonald had a farm, E-I-E-I-O.

And on her farm she had a Hyena, E-I-E-I-O,
With a Whee-Hee here and a Whee-Hee there,
   (*Slap leg with hand while laughing.*)
Here a Whee, there a Hee,
Everywhere a Whee-Hee,
Old MacDonald had a farm, E-I-E-I-O.

And on her farm she had an Iguana, E-I-E-I-O,
With a Gulp-Gulp here and a Gulp-Gulp there,
   (*Roll out tongue and slowly gulp.*)
Here a Gulp, there a Gulp,
Everywhere a Gulp-Gulp,
Old MacDonald had a farm, E-I-E-I-O.

And on her farm she had a Jaguar, E-I-E-I-O,
With a Growl-Growl here and a Growl-Growl
   there, (*Make a mean face and growl.*)
Here a Growl, there a Growl,
Everywhere a Growl-Growl,
Old MacDonald had a farm, E-I-E-I-O.

And on her farm she had a Kangaroo, E-I-E-I-O,
With a Hop-Hop here and a Hop-Hop there, (*Hop in place.*)
Here a Hop, there a Hop,
Everywhere a Hop-Hop,
Old MacDonald had a farm, E-I-E-I-O.

And on her farm she had a Llama, E-I-E-I-O,
With a Spit-Spit here and a Spit-Spit there, (*Don't
   actually spit, but make the spitting noise.*)
Here a Spit, there a Spit,

Everywhere a Spit-Spit,
Old MacDonald had a farm, E-I-E-I-O.

And on her farm she had a Monkey, E-I-E-I-O,
With an Ooh-Ooh here and an Ooh-Ooh there, (*Hold
    hands overhead while making the noise.*)
Here an Ooh, there an Ooh,
Everywhere an Ooh-Ooh,
Old MacDonald had a farm, E-I-E-I-O.

And on her farm she had a Narwhal, E-I-E-I-O,
With a Grunt-Grunt here and a Grunt-Grunt there, (*Hold arm out on
    head like a long horn. A narwhal makes a short, sharp grunt.*)
Here a Grunt, there a Grunt,
Everywhere a Grunt-Grunt,
Old MacDonald had a farm, E-I-E-I-O.

And on her farm she had an Octopus, E-I-E-I-O,
With a Hug-Hug here and a Hug-Hug there, (*Hug yourself.*)
Here a Hug, there a Hug,
Everywhere a Hug-Hug,
Old MacDonald had a farm, E-I-E-I-O.

And on her farm she had a Penguin, E-I-E-I-O,
With a Waddle-Waddle here and a Waddle-Waddle
    there, (*Waddle in a tight circle.*)
Here a Waddle, there a Waddle,
Everywhere a Waddle-Waddle,
Old MacDonald had a farm, E-I-E-I-O.

And on her farm she had a Quail, E-I-E-I-O,
With a Bob-WHITE here and a Bob-WHITE there, (*Bob head
    up and down and emphasize* WHITE *on the call.*)
Here a Bob, there a Bob,
Everywhere a Bob-WHITE,
Old MacDonald had a farm, E-I-E-I-O.

And on her farm she had a Rattlesnake, E-I-E-I-O,
With a Shake-Shake here and a Shake-Shake
 there, (*Shake fist to simulate a rattle.*)
Here a Shake, there a Shake,
Everywhere a Shake-Shake,
Old MacDonald had a farm, E-I-E-I-O.

And on her farm she had a Seal, E-I-E-I-O,
With an Orp-Orp here and an Orp-Orp there, (*Clap the
 back of your hands in front of your body.*)
Here an Orp, there an Orp,
Everywhere an Orp-Orp,
Old MacDonald had a farm, E-I-E-I-O.

And on her farm she had a Trumpeter Swan, E-I-E-I-O,
With a Honk-Honk here and a Honk-Honk there,
 (*Stretch neck while honking.*)
Here a Honk, there a Honk,
Everywhere a Honk-Honk,
Old MacDonald had a farm, E-I-E-I-O.

And on her farm she had a Ural Owl, E-I-E-I-O,
With a Whoo-Whoo here and a Whoo-Whoo there,
 (*Blink and turn head around while hooting.*)
Here a Whoo, there a Whoo,
Everywhere a Whoo-Whoo,
Old MacDonald had a farm, E-I-E-I-O.

And on her farm she had a Vulture, E-I-E-I-O,
With a Soar-Soar here and a Soar-Soar there, (*Hold
 arms out as wings and move in a circle.*)
Here a Soar, there a Soar,
Everywhere a Soar-Soar,
Old MacDonald had a farm, E-I-E-I-O.

And on her farm she had a Wolf, E-I-E-I-O,
With a Howl-Howl here and a Howl-Howl there, (*Lift head back to howl.*)

Here a Howl, there a Howl,
Everywhere a Howl-Howl,
Old MacDonald had a farm, E-I-E-I-O.

And on her farm she had a Xenarthra (*Stop and explain*
that a sloth is a member of the suborder Xenarthra,
pronounced "ZEN-are-thra."), E-I-E-I-O,
With a Snore-Snore here and a Snore-Snore there, (*Close eyes*
and hold hands overhead as if grasping a branch.)
Here a Snore, there a Snore,
Everywhere a Snore-Snore,
Old MacDonald had a farm, E-I-E-I-O.

And on her farm she had a Yak, E-I-E-I-O,
With a Snort-Snort here and a Snort-Snort there, (*Shake head and chew.*)
Here a Snort, there a Snort,
Everywhere a Snort-Snort,
Old MacDonald had a farm, E-I-E-I-O.

(*Spoken*): Wait!
Old MacDonald didn't have a farm.
She had a ZOO! (*Slap forehead.*)

Picture Book

Van Fleet, Matthew. *Alphabet.* Simon and Schuster, 2008.

This toy book has a lot of tactile features (furry tails, scaly skin); lift-the-flaps; and pull-tabs. Like "Old MacDonald ABC," this book features several exotic animals, from alligators to zorillas (a polecat). There is also a key in the back matter that asks the children to locate other animals on each page.

Storytelling Tip: Read the entire book and then allow the children some time to explore the various aspects of the book.

Closing Activity

Library Alphabet Scavenger Hunt.

As the children leave the story-program area, ask them to look around the library. (We limit them to the children's area.) Point out different items in the library. Then tape homemade or commercially made letters to each item. Don't worry about trying to find an object for each letter. Many letters will have more than one related object, so have extra letters on hand. Some items are obvious. Some can be strategically placed books. We bought several children's-book-character plush toys for display. Walk around with the children. The moms and dads usually help at this point. When you have put the last letter on, ask the children to look at how funny all of the letters in the library look. This usually elicits several laughs from them.

Here are some ideas:

A almanacs, Amelia Bedelia books, Arthur books, atlases
B bathrooms, books, bookmarks
C *The Cat in the Hat*, chairs, children, compact discs, computers, Curious George books
D dictionaries, doors, Dr. Seuss books
E books about elephants, encyclopedias
F fairy tales, Fancy Nancy books, fish, floor
G games, Grimm's fairy tales
H Halloween books, Harry Potter books
I *If You Give a Mouse a Cookie*, information desk, books about insects
J joke books
K books about kangaroos, keyboards, kids
L librarians
M magazines, Mother Goose books, movies
N newspapers, nursery rhyme books
O Olivia books, books about owls, orange books
P paintings, posters, puppets, puzzles
Q books about queens
R books about rabbits, Rainbow Fish books
S shelves, story area/room
T tables, Thomas the Tank Engine books
U books about unicorns
V *The Very Hungry Caterpillar*

W   walls, *Where the Wild Things Are,* windows

X   We put up an "*X* marks the spot" wall display simply so we could
      have a visible *X*.

Y   books with yellow covers, *Yertle the Turtle and Other Stories*

Z   books about zebras

Consider Substituting These Picture Books

Catalanotto, Peter. *Matthew A.B.C.* Atheneum, 2002.

Mrs. Tuttle has twenty-five students named Matthew in her classroom. Each Matthew has a distinct personality trait associated with a different letter of the alphabet.
The funniest of these are Matthew J, who works a night job, and Matthew T, who is
fiercely tense. The oddest is Matthew F, who has a cat on his face. At the end of the
book, Matthew Z, the new student, arrives with clothing covered with zippers.

Storytelling Tip: Different Matthews show up in the background illustrations before
they are featured. Take the time to flip the pages back and forth to locate them.

Grossman, Bill. *My Little Sister Hugged an Ape.*
Illustrated by Kevin Hawkes. Knopf, 2004.

The narrator's goofy sister is on a hugging spree and goes after an alphabetical array
of animals. When she squeezes the ape, it lets out a burp. After she hugs a tiny bug, it
flies up her nose. And when she hugs a cow, it squirts milk all over. One of the more
comical hugs comes with the letter *R*. Sister hugs a rat. It goes flat, so she blows in
its ear to fill it up with air so she can hug it again. Also, when Sister hugs the zebra,
the stripes aren't dry, and Sister wears them instead. In the end, the little sister is
"hugging ME!"

Storytelling Tip: Grossman's verse naturally lends itself to vocal and facial exag-
gerations by the reader. Follow your instincts as well as Sister's expressions.

Horowitz, Dave. *Twenty-Six Princesses.* Putnam, 2008.

Apparently, the prince is a frog. Twenty-six different princesses (each one's name
beginning with a different letter of the alphabet) make their way to his castle. Princess
Alice is the first one to the palace, Princess Betty is "still getting ready," and Princess
Criss tries to steal a kiss.

Storytelling Tip: As you read the book, have the children mime what the princesses are doing. Some actions will be fairly vague, and that's OK; just plow ahead.

Some won't be obvious what to mime, but be creative. For example, Princess Alice arrives first—simply hold up one finger. Let the illustrations help. Princess Betty is still getting dressed. The picture shows her pulling a sweater over her head. Simply mime that. Other ideas include Princess Lori, not in the story (simply look around and shrug your shoulders); Princess Vikki, who is very tricky (make an "OK" sign with your fingers); and Princess Zaire, who is finally there (have everyone make a "ta-da" sound and gesture).

Kontis, Alethea. *Alpha Oops! The Day Z Went First.*
Illustrated by Bob Kolar. Candlewick, 2006.

There are a handful of alphabet books where the *Z* is predominant. This is the best one. As the book starts out, with "A is for Apple," Z bursts into the scene and states, "Zebra and I are SICK of this last-in-line stuff! This time we want to go first!" Some of the middle letters decide to go out of order, too. Because *A* is going last, she makes a grand production. The companion book is titled *Alpha Oops! H Is for Halloween* (Candlewick, 2010).

Storytelling Tip: This is a good time for alphabet refrigerator magnets and a metal sheet to hold them on. Have them placed in correct order at the beginning of the storytelling. Move them around as the letters in the book take up their new order. See what the new alphabetical lineup looks like by the end of the book. You can also use paper letters with tape, felt letters on a felt board, or letters with Velcro backings on a cloth board.

ZOO-LARIOUS!

Program at a Glance

Opening Picture Book: *Wild about Books* by Judy Sierra and Marc Brown

Movement Activity: "Doot Doot Zoo," traditional, with new words by Rob Reid

Picture Book: *Pssst!* by Adam Rex

Song: "Mary Had a Little Zoo," traditional, with new words by Rob Reid

Picture Book: *Felicity Floo Visits the Zoo* by E. S. Redmond

Picture Book: *Who Ate All the Cookie Dough?* by Karen Beaumont and Eugene Yelchin

Fingerplay: "Five Little Monkeys Swinging in the Zoo," traditional, with new words by Rob Reid

Picture Book: *Penguins* by Liz Pichon

Closing Movement Activity: "The Penguin March" by Rob Reid

Opening Picture Book

Sierra, Judy. *Wild about Books*. Illustrated by Marc Brown. Knopf, 2004.

A librarian accidentally drives the bookmobile into the zoo. She begins reading a Dr. Seuss book, and several curious zoo animals decide to investigate. The library books prove to be a big hit with the animals. Not only do they find good titles to read, but the librarian also teaches them to take care of the books. The animals move from reading books to writing their own. In the end, the animals build a "Zoobrary."

Storytelling Tip: Even though some of the inside illustrated jokes will be over your young audience members' heads, read a select few to the delight of any adult sitting in the story program. One example shows a llama munching on grass while reading *The Grass Menagerie*.

Movement Activity

"Doot Doot Zoo," traditional, with new words by Rob Reid.

I got this idea from the popular traditional camp activity "Baby Shark." Simply chant the words while making the motions. Yell the word *zoo* louder than the other words.

> Rattlesnake! Doot, doot, doot, doot, doot, zoo!
> Rattlesnake! Doot, doot, doot, doot, doot, zoo!
> (*Hold up fist as if it were the rattle of the snake's tail and shake it.*)

> Chimpanzee! Doot, doot, doot, doot, doot, zoo!
> Chimpanzee! Doot, doot, doot, doot, doot, zoo!
> (*Hold arms up overhead and sway back and forth.*)

> Crocodile! Doot, doot, doot, doot, doot, zoo!
> Crocodile! Doot, doot, doot, doot, doot, zoo!
> (*Move arms up and down as crocodile jaws.*)

> Kangaroo! Doot, doot, doot, doot, doot, zoo!
> Kangaroo! Doot, doot, doot, doot, doot, zoo!
> (*Hop in place.*)

Mountain Goat! Doot, doot, doot, doot, doot, zoo!
Mountain Goat! Doot, doot, doot, doot, doot, zoo!
(*Make horns with fingers.*)

Polar Bear! Doot, doot, doot, doot, doot, zoo!
Polar Bear! Doot, doot, doot, doot, doot, zoo!
(*Put one "paw" in front of the other and sway side to side.*)

Elephant! Doot, doot, doot, doot, doot, zoo!
Elephant! Doot, doot, doot, doot, doot, ZOO!
(*Hold arm in front of nose like a trunk and give a loud, last "ZOO!"*)

Picture Book

Rex, Adam. *Pssst!* Harcourt, 2007.

While a girl is visiting a zoo, the various animals make the "pssst" sound and ask her to purchase specific items. When she asks how she is to pay for everything, a baboon hands her a bag of coins, and a tortoise informs her, "The peacock picks them out of the fountain."

Storytelling Tip: Read a few select signs for any adult audience members. One of the signs is at the walrus exhibit and reads, "I Am the Walrus (koo-koo-kachoo)." Also—cue your young audience members to make the "pssst" sound at the appropriate times in the book. Cue them with a nod of the head.

Song

"Mary Had a Little Zoo," traditional, with new words by Rob Reid.

Mary had a little zoo, little zoo, little zoo,
Mary had a little zoo, she had a little zoo.
And in her zoo, she had a giraffe, had a giraffe, had a giraffe,
And in her zoo, she had a giraffe, it looked a lot like this . . .
(*Have children act out what they think a giraffe should look like. In
many instances, they stand up and stretch their arms up high.*)

And in her zoo, she had a hippo, had a hippo, had a hippo,
And in her zoo, she had a hippo, it looked a lot like this . . .
(*The kids usually open their mouths wide.*)

And in her zoo, she had a rhino, had a rhino, had a rhino,
And in her zoo, she had a rhino, it looked a lot like this . . .
(*Hold forearm and hand in front of nose for the rhino's horn.*)

(*Add any other zoo animal you think the kids would have some
success acting like. Let them be creative and come up with
their own ideas. There are no right or wrong responses.*)

Picture Book

Redmond, E. S. *Felicity Floo Visits the Zoo.*
Candlewick, 2009.

All of the animals in the zoo are sick. The zookeeper has no idea how this happened
all at once. We, however, learn that little Felicity Floo came to the zoo and "wiped
her red, runny nose without a tissue." She then proceeds to touch the various animals,
leaving "green, gloppy goo" on them. The book ends with the following caution: "Her
cold got so big / That they called it The Floo / You may not believe me, / But if I were
you, / I think I'd go bowling / And not to the zoo."

   Storytelling Tip: After Felicity touches each animal and leaves behind her green
goo, have the kids say in unison, "Eeyooh." More times than not, I *haven't* had to cue
the kids to say this beforehand.

Picture Book

Beaumont, Karen. *Who Ate All the Cookie Dough?*
Illustrated by Eugene Yelchin. Holt, 2008.

Mother Kangaroo is on the trail to find out who ate the cookie dough. She asks a lion
cub, and this starts off a chain of denials. "I don't know, / It wasn't me. / Maybe Zebra,
/ Let's go see . . ." Mother Kangaroo also asks Llama, Cheetah, Hippo, and Monkey.
Everyone finally learns that Baby Kangaroo has been eating the cookie dough while
hiding in his mama's pouch.

Storytelling Tip: This cumulative tale can be easily transformed into a felt story with patterns taken from either coloring books or animal pages from the Internet. You can also cue the kids to put their slightly cupped hands over their eyes as if to shield them from the sun on the animals' line, "Let's go see . . ."

Fingerplay

"Five Little Monkeys Swinging in the Zoo," traditional, with new words by Rob Reid.

Five little monkeys swinging in the zoo, (*Make
   overhead arm-over-arm swinging motion.*)
One escaped and bid "Adieu!" (*Blow a kiss.*)
Call the keeper—here's what she'll do, (*Hold thumb
   and pinkie by ear as if talking into phone.*)
She'll say, "Lock that cage (*Make twisting motion
   with hand as if turning a key in a lock.*)
When they're swinging in the zoo!" (*Shake finger as if scolding.*)

Four little monkeys swinging in the zoo, (*Make
   overhead arm-over-arm swinging motion.*)
One escaped and bid "Adieu!" (*Blow a kiss.*)
Call the keeper—here's what she'll do, (*Hold thumb
   and pinkie by ear as if talking into phone.*)
She'll say, "Lock that cage (*Make twisting motion
   with hand as if turning a key in a lock.*)
When they're swinging in the zoo!" (*Shake finger as if scolding.*)

Three little monkeys swinging in the zoo, (*Make
   overhead arm-over-arm swinging motion.*)
One escaped and bid "Adieu!" (*Blow a kiss.*)
Call the keeper—here's what she'll do, (*Hold thumb
   and pinkie by ear as if talking into phone.*)
She'll say, "Lock that cage (*Make twisting motion
   with hand as if turning a key in a lock.*)
When they're swinging in the zoo!" (*Shake finger as if scolding.*)

Two little monkeys swinging in the zoo, (*Make
     overhead arm-over-arm swinging motion.*)
One escaped and bid "Adieu!" (*Blow a kiss.*)
Call the keeper—here's what she'll do, (*Hold thumb
     and pinkie by ear as if talking into phone.*)
She'll say, "Lock that cage (*Make twisting motion
     with hand as if turning a key in a lock.*)
When they're swinging in the zoo!" (*Shake finger as if scolding.*)

One little monkey swinging in the zoo (*Make
     overhead arm-over-arm swinging motion.*)
He escaped and bid "Adieu!" (*Blow a kiss.*)
Call the keeper—here's what she'll do, (*Hold thumb
     and pinkie by ear as if talking into phone.*)
She'll say,
(*Spoken*) "I guess we can go home now." (*Shrug shoulders.*)

Picture Book

Pichon, Liz. *Penguins.* Orchard, 2008.

One day at the zoo, when all the people are gone for the day, the penguins discover
a camera left behind. They start taking pictures of each other. "Everyone look at me
and say FISH!" After a while, the camera stops working, and the penguins leave it
alone. The zookeeper spots it the next day and finds the proper owner, a little girl.
When her pictures are developed, the little girl notices an unusual number of penguin
pictures. The book itself comes with an accordion-style insert full of penguin pictures.

Storytelling Tip: At the end of the story, ask the children to walk around the story
area like penguins and take actual pictures of them. Be sure to ask them to say "FISH!"
instead of the traditional "CHEESE!"

Closing Movement Activity

"The Penguin March" by Rob Reid.

Recite the following cadence while the children march like penguins around the room.
Say the "Hup-two-three-four" lines as many times as you need for them to circle the
room a few times and then head toward the exit.

The penguin march,
A waddling march,
Hup-two-three-four
Hup-two-three-four
Hup-two-three-four
Waddle, waddle, out the door.

Consider Substituting These Picture Books

Bardhan-Quallen, Sudipta. *Quackenstein Hatches a Family.*
Illustrated by Brian T. Jones. Abrams, 2010.

"In the darkest corner of the zoo there stood a gloomy shack. A nearby scrawl read: Keep Out All. Just Leave Me Be! Signed, Quack." Quackenstein the duck is bitter because he doesn't have a little one to care for. One day, he grabs an orphaned egg and puts it in his nest. When the egg hatches, Quack is afraid a monster will emerge. He runs all over the zoo to escape the creature. The "monster" turns out to be a baby platypus, who calls Quack "Daddy." "And off they walked, in step, and paw in wing."

Storytelling Tip: When the egg starts cracking, Quack blurts out, "IT'S ALIVE!" Use your best Boris Karloff or Vincent Price voice to deliver this line.

Pinkwater, Daniel. *Bad Bears in the Big City.*
Illustrated by Jill Pinkwater. Houghton Mifflin, 2003.

Two polar bears, Irving and Muktuk, arrive at the zoo—in chains. "They are not to be trusted." They are shown to their rooms, and they meet their roommate, Roy, "the other polar bear." Roy has an apartment he goes to each night. The three of them eat bear chow but long for muffins from the nearby muffin factory. One night, after Roy checks out (we see him at a time clock), Irving and Muktuk plan their escape. They eventually disguise themselves and join a tour at the muffin factory. They are in trouble for leaving the zoo, but Roy promises to watch them. "They are bad bears, I have to say it . . . But they have assured me they will not eat people."

Storytelling Tip: Pinkwater's humor style is a "deadpan humor"—a bit droll and funny but delivered with a straight face. Read it that way. And if you want to serve muffins to your audience afterward . . .

Waldron, Kevin. *Mr. Peek and the Misunderstanding at the Zoo.* **Templar, 2008.**

When Mr. Peek goes on his rounds, one of his jacket buttons pops off. He says to himself, "Oh, woe is me! You're getting very fat . . ." The hippo overhears and thinks the remark is intended for her! During his rounds, Mr. Peek makes several other statements to himself, and several other animals believe he is talking about them. His son, Jimmy, informs Mr. Peek, "You have MY jacket on, Dad!" They swap jackets, and Mr. Peek runs around making new statements that, luckily, erase the other misheard words. The animals are delighted.

Storytelling Tip: Contrast the voice of Mr. Peek when he's feeling sorry for himself with a livelier vocal delivery once he realizes he isn't gaining weight.

Watson, Benjamin James. *The Boy Who Went Ape.* Illustrated by Richard Jesse Watson. Blue Sky, 2008.

Benjamin has always gotten in trouble with his teacher, Ms. Thunderbum. "But the most trouble he ever got in was the day his class went on a field trip around town. The first stop was the zoo." Benjamin walks into a cage. A chimpanzee grabs Benjamin's cap, jacket, and backpack and locks up the boy. Everyone mistakes the chimp for Benjamin. The class continues on to the library (the chimp yells), the grocery store (the chimp starts a food fight), and the bank (the chimp stops a robbery). Meanwhile, Benjamin is having a blast playing with the other chimpanzees.

Storytelling Tip: After you read the book, share the dedications from this father-son team with your audience. "For Ben: Ever since we brought you home from the zoo, you have been like a son to us." "And thanks, Dad, for the cool pictures—not bad for a knuckle-walker."

PART **2**

HUMOR PROGRAMS FOR THE SCHOOL-AGE CROWD

BOO HA-HA

Program at a Glance

Opening Poem: "Teeny Tiny Ghost" by Lilian Moore
from *Beware, Take Care: Fun and Spooky Poems*

Jokes and Riddles: Selections by Paul Brewer from *You Must Be Joking*

Picture Book: *I'm Not Afraid of This Haunted House*
by Laurie Friedman and Teresa Murfin

Chapter Book Selection: "Anything You Want" from *Invasion of the
Road Weenies and Other Warped and Creepy Tales* by David Lubar

Picture Book: *Dear Vampa* by Ross Collins

Poem: "Mary Had a Vampire Bat" by Judy Sierra from *Monster Goose*

Picture Book: *A Vampire Is Coming to Dinner!* by
Pamela Jane and Pedro Rodriguez

Picture Book/Musical Activity: *If You're a Monster and You Know It* by
Rebecca Emberley and Ed Emberley, with new verses by Rob Reid

Closing Picture Book: *Twelve Terrible Things* by Marty Kelley

Opening Poem

Moore, Lilian. "Teeny Tiny Ghost," from *Beware, Take Care: Fun and Spooky Poems.* Holt, 2006.

Set the tone of the program by reciting this poem in an overly dramatic voice. The narrator talks about a ghost no bigger than a mouse. Build up to the last line: "If you stood and listened right, / You'd hear a / Teeny / Tiny / BOO!"

Storytelling Tip: For comedic effect, pause before the final word, and say it with a contrasting high-pitched and soft delivery.

Jokes and Riddles

Brewer, Paul. *You Must Be Joking.* Cricket, 2003.

Sprinkle jokes and riddles from the chapter titled "Hairy and Scary" throughout the program. Sample riddles include, "What did the Hunchback of Notre Dame do after he brushed his teeth? He gargoyled."

Picture Book

Friedman, Laurie. *I'm Not Afraid of This Haunted House.* Illustrated by Teresa Murfin. Carolrhoda, 2005.

A young boy bravely leads his small group of friends into a haunted house, where they encounter a scary cast of characters, from a witch to a one-eyed monster. The final pages build up the tension as Simon crawls into a coffin, sticks a toe into a pool of blood, walks through a pitch-black room, and balances on a moving floor. His friends have the final laugh when Simon loudly proclaims, "I'M NOT AFRAID OF THIS . . . EEEEEEEEEEEEEEK . . . A MOUSE!"

Storytelling Tip: Have the audience chime along with the narrator's repetitive brag: "I'm Simon Lester Henry Strauss, and I'm not afraid of this haunted house."

Chapter Book Selection

Lubar, David. "Anything You Want," from *Invasion of the Road Weenies and Other Warped and Creepy Tales.* Starscape, 2005.

Three-year-old Stevie and his older sister, the narrator, find a magic bottle. A genie pops out and grants Stevie three wishes. His sister tries to help, but the genie shushes her. Unfortunately, Stevie doesn't talk clearly. His first wish is for peas (he really likes to eat them). The genie misunderstands and grants him world peace for one hundred years. Stevie's second wish is "Liver . . . Never." Stevie never wants to eat liver again. The genie hears "Live forever" and grants Stevie immortality. Stevie then decides to let his sister get in on the fun. He states, "Sissie wish." The genie turns the sister into a fish.

Picture Book

Collins, Ross. *Dear Vampa.* HarperCollins, 2009.

A family of vampires, drawn in black and white, are dismayed by their new neighbors, drawn in full color, who appear to be normal humans. When the vampires try to sleep during the day, the new neighbors—the Wolfsons—are making noise. The vampires are disgusted by the fact that the Wolfsons lie out in the sun. The new neighbor children don't seem to warm up to the vampire's pet, Cuddles, a large creature with tentacles. The funniest scene is when the vampire father is drinking what he thinks is a glass of blood. He spits it out when he realizes it is tomato juice. The vampires pack up their things and move back to stay with Vampa, in Transylvania.

Storytelling Tip: Pause as you hold the double-page spread of the Wolfson family watching the vampires moving. There are some subtle visual clues that lead to the surprise ending.

Poem

Sierra, Judy. "Mary Had a Vampire Bat," from *Monster Goose.* Harcourt, 2001.

Instead of a lamb, Mary has a vampire bat that follows her to school.

Storytelling Tip: Although the poem isn't written out in full lyric format, you can easily adapt every other line and sing it to the traditional tune of "Mary Had a Little Lamb." For example, the first two lines of the poem are printed as "Mary had a vampire bat. / His fur was black as night." Sing it as "Mary had a vampire bat, vampire bat, vampire bat. / Mary had a vampire bat. / His fur was black as night." The teacher eventually screams, and school is cancelled ("Just as Mary planned").

Picture Book

Jane, Pamela. *A Vampire Is Coming to Dinner!*
Illustrated by Pedro Rodriguez. Price Stern Sloan, 2010.

A boy is shocked to learn that a vampire has invited himself over to dinner. The book has a list of rules that the boy supplements with creative spins. For example, the third rule is "Put out a welcome mat." We lift the flap to see that the boy is rigging a can of paint over the doorway. Another rule is "Be sure to put the cat out. Vampires and cats don't get along." The picture under the flap shows the vampire sitting on a couch covered in cats.

Storytelling Tip: After reading each rule, lift the flap to reveal the corresponding picture and pause long enough to let the audience members get a nice long look.

Picture Book/Musical Activity

Emberley, Rebecca. *If You're a Monster and You Know It.* own
Illustrated by Ed Emberley. Orchard, 2010. New verses by Rob Reid.

The Emberleys have made a silly, scary version of the traditional song "If You're Happy and You Know It." New verses encourage the children to act like monsters and "snort and growl," "smack your claws," "stomp your paws," "twitch your tail," "wiggle your warts," "give a roar," and "do it all."

Storytelling Tip: Hold up the Emberleys' picture book, and sing a couple verses from the book. Point out that the picture book, although it is a lot of fun, is aimed at a younger crowd and that everyone should brainstorm a version appropriate for older elementary kids. Here are three verses to get them started. Have everyone stand, sing, and move to the lyrics.

> If you're a monster and you know it, make a face, (*Have
>   everyone look at each other while making a creepy face.*)
> If you're a monster and you know it, make a face,
> If you're a monster and you know it,
> And you really want to show it,
> If you're a monster and you know it, make a face.

If you're a monster and you know it, walk like a zombie,
  (*Have everyone shuffle around the room.*)
If you're a monster and you know it, walk like a zombie,
If you're a monster and you know it,
And you really want to show it,
If you're a monster and you know it, walk like a zombie.

If you're a monster and you know it, howl like a werewolf,
  (*Everyone throws back his or her head and howls.*)
If you're a monster and you know it, howl like a werewolf.
If you're a monster and you know it,
And you really want to show it,
If you're a monster and you know it, howl like a werewolf.

If time allows, ask the kids for more suggestions and act those out.

Closing Picture Book

Kelley, Marty. *Twelve Terrible Things.* **Tricycle Press, 2008.**

The author gives us a series of child's-point-of-view images of supposedly terrible things. These are ice cream falling off a cone; octopus tentacles coming up from under your bed; a dentist; a bad haircut; an old woman reaching out to pinch your cheeks; a clown at a birthday party; a long, long, long car ride; a goldfish being flushed down a toilet; the top of a high dive at a swimming pool; school cafeteria food; and socks being stuck under your nose. The last picture shows the twelfth "terrible thing"—an ice-cream cone being handed to you with the word "Yeaaaaah!"

Storytelling Tip: Have the kids scream loudly every time you show them one of the "terrible things." The screams add to the comedic effect.

Consider Substituting These Picture Books

McElligott, Matthew. *Even Monsters Get Haircuts.* **Walker, 2010.**

A boy sneaks into his father's barbershop in the middle of the night accompanied by a vampire. He then cuts the hair of a variety of monsters, including a Cyclops, Frankenstein's monster, Medusa (the boy is wearing a blindfold while working on her), and a skeleton (the boy is shown looking puzzled at the skeleton's skull). Everyone is surprised when a human customer enters—until the customer removes his head. "We all had a good laugh over that one."

Storytelling Tip: Be sure to emphasize the fact that the boy opens the shop with a skeleton key by pausing one beat, and giving the audience a funny look, after reading that line. Use the same reading technique when he unpacks his supplies: "rotting tonic, horn polish, stick wax, and shamp-*ewww*."

Noll, Amanda. *I Need My Monster.*
Illustrated by Howard McWilliam. Flashlight Press, 2009.

One night, a boy finds a note from the monster under his bed. It reads, "Gone fishing. Back in a week. Gabe." The boy auditions other monsters. The first monster doesn't have claws. "But I have an overbite. And I'm a mouth breather." The second monster has claws, but there's nail polish on them. "I believe professional monsters should always be well-groomed." The third monster turns out to be a girl monster wearing a pink bow on her tail. "Boy monsters are for boys and girl monsters are for girls," says our protagonist. The next monster has a long, silly-looking tongue that makes the boy laugh. Gabe finally returns, ready to scare his boy again. "I shivered again. I'd be asleep in no time."

Storytelling Tip: Have fun playing with the voices of the various monsters. The mouth-breathing monster has a pathetic panting sound, like "Hih-huh, hih-huh." The well-groomed monster can have a snobbish voice. Read the first lines each monster says in a scary voice, and once the boy calls them out, revert to a contrasting silly voice.

Pulver, Robin. *Never Say Boo!* Illustrated by Deb Lucke. Holiday House, 2009.

Gordon, the new kid in school, is actually a ghost. His teacher and classmates are terrified, but everyone carries on. Unfortunately, whenever he says a word that contains a "boo" sound, like the teacher's name, Miss Boodle, the situation gets worse. Gordon refrains from answering questions such as "I am thinking of an object from Australia that can be thrown so that it returns to the thrower. Who knows what it is?" (A boomerang.) A fire breaks out in school and the fire alarms don't work. Gordon becomes a hero when his ghostly moan brings the firefighters to the scene.

Storytelling Tip: Ask your audience at this point to make a loud, drawn-out "boo" to help attract the attention of the firefighters.

Schaefer, Lola M. *Frankie Stein.*
Illustrated by Kevan Atteberry. Marshall Cavendish, 2007.

Anyone who knows the 1960s television show *The Munsters* will appreciate this book. A normal child is born to a mother who looks like the bride of Frankenstein, and to a father who looks like Frankenstein's monster. The parents try to make their son, Frankie, as scary as the rest of the family, but the boy is too human to pull it off. Finally, Frankie makes "a grand appearance," looking well-groomed and wearing clean clothes. His parents are frightened and faint "dead away." Everyone agrees that Frankie is "the scariest Stein of all."

Storytelling Tip: Have the kids in your audience shriek and pretend to faint to the ground at the same time Frankie's parents faint in the book.

Taylor, Sean. *When a Monster Is Born.* ᵦᵤᵐ
Illustrated by Nick Sharratt. Roaring Brook, 2007.

Life is a series of options, even for monsters. "When a monster is born . . . there are two possibilities—either it's a FARAWAY-IN-THE-FORESTS monster, or . . . it's an UNDER-YOUR-BED monster." If it turns out to be the under-your-bed type, it will either eat you or be your friend and go to school with you. The funny scenario is played out all the way to the possibility of two monsters falling in love and either having a baby or eating each other. And, of course, the baby could turn out to be "a FARAWAY-IN-THE-FORESTS monster, or . . . an UNDER-YOUR-BED monster."

Storytelling Tip: Every time the phrase "there are two possibilities" comes up (and it does quite often in this book), hold up two fingers. Eventually, your audience will chime in with you.

FUNNY BUNNY

Program at a Glance

Opening Picture Book: *Rescue Bunnies* by Doreen Cronin and Scott Menchin

Picture Book: *Muncha! Muncha! Muncha!* by Candace Fleming and G. Brian Karas

Fingerplay: "A Rabbit" by Rob Reid

Picture Book: *Knuffle Bunny Too: A Case of Mistaken Identity* by Mo Willems

Movement Activity: "There Were Ten Bunnies Hopping" by Rob Reid

Picture Book: *A Boy and His Bunny* by Sean Bryan and Tom Murphy

Musical Activity: "My Bunny Hops into Its Burrow,"
traditional, with new words by Rob Reid

Closing Picture Book: *Duck! Rabbit!* by Amy Krouse Rosenthal
and Tom Lichtenheld

Opening Picture Book

Cronin, Doreen. *Rescue Bunnies.*
Illustrated by Scott Menchin. HarperCollins, 2010.

"Newbie is a Rescue Bunny trainee." She goes out on a mission with her team to rescue a baby giraffe from a mud hole. They have to move fast because a pack of hyenas is headed their way. They are unable to pull the giraffe out. The rescue team is ready to leave, but Newbie sticks by the giraffe. The team tries it once more, and they succeed just in time.

Storytelling Tip: The book is full of classic lines from movies. These include "Surely you can't be serious. I am serious . . . and don't call me Shirley"; "You can't handle the truth"; "You had me at hello"; "I'm king of the world"; and "Here's looking at you, kid." Try to deliver the lines like they are delivered in the movies. If nothing else, give the last line your best Humphrey Bogart.

Picture Book

Fleming, Candace. *Muncha! Muncha! Muncha!*
Illustrated by G. Brian Karas. Atheneum, 2002.

Mr. McGreely is tired of three rabbits eating his garden vegetables. He builds a small wire fence around the garden, but that doesn't stop the rabbits. He then builds a tall wooden wall around the garden. The rabbits still get in. Mr. McGreely becomes "really, really angry." He digs a deep, wet trench around the garden. The rabbits swim the trench, climb the wall, and hop over the fence to eat the vegetables. Mr. McGreely builds an enormous fortress around his garden. The rabbits are stumped at first, but they sneak into his basket when he picks the vegetables.

Storytelling Tip: Teach your audience some movements and sound effects before you read the book to them. When they hear "Tippy-Tippy-Tippy, Pat," they should move their fingers as if walking. When they hear "Muncha! Muncha! Muncha!" they should mime eating. For the phrase "Spring-hurdle, Dash! Dash! Dash!" the children should move their hands as if jumping over a hurdle and then pump their arms as if they were running. When they hear "Dig-scrabble, Scratch! Scratch! Scratch!" they should pretend to dig with their hands. Finally, for "Dive-paddle, Splash! Splash! Splash!" have the children make swimming motions.

Fingerplay

"A Rabbit" by Rob Reid.

The children should stand for this fingerplay.

> A rabbit has two long ears, (*Hold up two fingers*
>   *behind your head for bunny ears.*)
> A rabbit has a wiggly nose, (*Wiggle your nose.*)
> A rabbit has a bushy tail, (*Tap your backside.*)
> That shakes wherever he goes. (*Shake bottom.*)

Picture Book

Willems, Mo. *Knuffle Bunny Too: A Case of Mistaken Identity.* Hyperion, 2007.

Trixie takes her stuffed Knuffle Bunny to school. She is upset to see that another girl, Sonja, has a Knuffle Bunny, too (even though they pronounce the word *Knuffle* differently). Their teacher takes the bunnies away from the girls and returns them when it's time to go home. In the middle of the night, Trixie realizes she has the wrong Knuffle Bunny. As she is trying to convince her father to fix the problem, they get a phone call from Sonja's father. The two fathers and two girls exchange bunnies in the middle of the night. Trixie and Sonja become best friends.

Storytelling Tip: A plush Knuffle Bunny toy is available on Mo Willems's website: www.mowillems.com. Buy two of them, and move them around as you read the story.

Movement Activity

"There Were Ten Bunnies Hopping" by Rob Reid.

Ask for a volunteer to stand in front of the group, hold up all ten fingers, and move them as if they were hopping bunnies. Recite the fingerplay verse.

> There were ten bunnies hopping,
> Hopping all around.
> There were ten bunnies hopping,
> Hopping safe and sound.

Ask for a second volunteer to join the first. Repeat the fingerplay with the new numbers.

> There were twenty bunnies hopping,
> Hopping all around.
> There were twenty bunnies hopping,
> Hopping safe and sound.

Repeat with as many children as want to volunteer. The highest number I got up to in a library setting was twelve volunteers, or "one hundred and twenty bunnies hopping." There were even more children who wanted to volunteer at this particular school family event, so I said, "Everyone stand." We then acted out, "There were MANY bunnies hopping, / Hopping all around. / There were MANY bunnies hopping, / Hopping safe and sound."

Picture Book

Bryan, Sean. *A Boy and His Bunny.* Illustrated by Tom Murphy. Arcade, 2005.

A boy wakes up to find a bunny on his head. He names the bunny Fred, and the two go about their day. The boy tells his mother, "You can do anything with a bunny on your head." Examples include spreading peanut butter, leading armies, and exploring the seabed "with a bunny on your head." The mother tells him that he looks cool with a bunny on his head. At that moment, the boy's sister walks in with an alligator on her head.

Storytelling Tip: Get a coworker to hold a stuffed bunny on your head while you read the story. It's too hard to turn the pages if you try to do it yourself. You'll look very silly reading the book with a bunny on your head. At the end of the story, hold up a copy of Bryan's sequel, *A Girl and Her Gator* (Arcade, 2006), and tell the children they can take turns reading *that* story after the program.

Musical Activity

"My Bunny Hops into Its Burrow," traditional, with new words by Rob Reid.

I took the camp-song version of "My Bonnie Lies over the Ocean" and wrote new verses to fit the theme of this story program. The camp version I learned instructs everyone in the audience to stand every time they sing a word beginning with the letter *B* and then to sit whenever they sing another word beginning with *B*. I came up with this idea while thinking of an activity that showcases the jumping ability of rabbits. Moving up and down simulates this motion. Go slow with young children, and do it with them so they know exactly when to stand and sit. One alternative activity is to have the audience members raise and lower their hands while sitting the whole time.

> My bunny hops into its burrow,
> My bunny hops wild and free,
> My bunny hops into its burrow,
> Oh, bring back my bunny to me.
> Bring back, bring back, oh, bring back my bunny to me, to me.
> Bring back, bring back, oh, bring back my bunny to me.

Closing Picture Book

Rosenthal, Amy Krouse. *Duck! Rabbit!* Illustrated by Tom Lichtenheld. Chronicle, 2009.

Each image in the book shows a creature that can be either a duck or a rabbit, depending which way one looks at it. One of the book's narrators sees something that appears to be the duck's bill. The other narrator sees it as the rabbit's ears. Each concedes that the other's observations might be right. At the end, they notice a creature that is either an anteater or a brachiosaurus.

Storytelling Tip: At the end of the book (and the story program), inform your audience that stories about an anteater or brachiosaurus will have to wait for another day. This is also a good picture book to read aloud with a partner.

Consider Substituting These Picture Books

Asher, Sandy. *Too Many Frogs!* Illustrated by Keith Graves. Philomel, 2005.

Rabbit likes living the simple life alone. One night, Froggie invites himself in to listen to Rabbit read a story. The next night, Froggie returns and makes himself a snack with Rabbit's food before listening to the story. Froggie returns a third night, and on the fourth night, he brings an entire Frog Family Reunion. Rabbit tells Froggie that "I never invited you in . . . And so I do mind. Very much indeed." But, as Rabbit reads his story, he realizes he misses Froggie. He opens the door to find the entire Frog Family Reunion on his steps. They were "waiting patiently to say they were sorry." Rabbit reads a story to all of them while wearing a "Frog Family Reunion" T-shirt.

Storytelling Tip: It's fun to read Froggie's dialogue with a low, drawn-out vocal treatment.

Czekaj, Jeff. *Hip and Hop Don't Stop.* Hyperion, 2010.

Hip is a rapping turtle, while Hop is a rapping rabbit. They become friends after they both spot a poster announcing the "Oldskool County First Annual Rap Off." Hip "rapped so slowly that everyone stopped paying attention." Hop rapped so fast that no one understood what she was saying. They learn that when they rap together, they get the whole crowd "breaking, popping, and locking to Hip and Hop's rhymes."

Storytelling Tip: The author provides clues on how to read the book right after the title page. The two rappers' raps are color coded. When you see Hop's green lines, read them fast. When you see Hip's red lines, read them slowly. The challenge will come when the two recite their four-line rap together. For added fun, throw in a "beat-box" mouth sound effect from time to time.

Klise, Kate. *Little Rabbit and the Meanest Mother on Earth.* Illustrated by Sarah Klise. Harcourt, 2010.

Little Rabbit is excited because the circus is in town. His mother states that he may go once his playroom is clean. He runs away and tells the ringmaster that he has "the Meanest Mother on Earth." He sells one hundred tickets for folks to see "this Mysterious Marvel of a Maternal Monstrosity." Rabbit leads his mother to the circus tent. The crowd is upset. "I want my money back." Mother tells them that she will show them something terrifying. She leads them all to her house and shows them Little Rabbit's messy playroom. "An Emporium of Odiferous Oddities!"

Storytelling Tip: When the ringmaster announces the mother, be sure to read his announcement with great ceremony, spreading your hands out. When mother shows the circus crowd her son's playroom, do the same.

Nyeu, Tao. *Bunny Days.* Dial, 2010.

Three very short stories follow a group of bunnies, their troubles, and how their friend Bear solves their problems. In "Muddy Bunnies," Mr. Goat splashes mud all over the bunnies. Bear pops them into the washing machine (delicate cycle, of course), then hangs the bunnies by their ears on the clothesline. The bunnies are sleeping deep underground in the second story, "Dusty Bunnies." Mrs. Goat accidentally sucks them up into her vacuum cleaner. Bear takes the bunnies out, places them in front of a big fan, and then repairs the vacuum cleaner. In the final story, "Bunny Tails," Mr. Goat accidentally shears off the bunnies' tails. Bear sews them back on. "Bear is very gentle."

Storytelling Tip: Read with a nonchalant voice to contrast the unusual circumstances of the stories. There are also a few sound-effect noises for the mud splash, the washing machine, the vacuum cleaner, a sneeze from the dust, the fan, and the sewing machine.

8

I READ IT IN A BOOK

Program at a Glance

Opening Picture Book: *Have I Got a Book for You* by Mélanie Watt

Rap: "The Rappin' Rob Rap (Version 3)" by Rob Reid

Picture Book: *Library Lion* by Michelle Knudsen and Kevin Hawkes

Chapter Book Selection: "The Test" from *The Legend of Spud Murphy* by Eoin Colfer

Picture Book: *Interrupting Chicken* by David Ezra Stein

Joke: "A Chicken Walks into a Library," traditional, adapted by Rob Reid

Readers' Theater: *Once upon a Motorcycle Dude* by Kevin O'Malley, Carol Heyer, and Scott Goto

Game: "Folklore Charades," traditional, adapted by Rob Reid

Closing Picture Book: *The Book That Eats People* by John Perry and Mark Fearing

Setup

The first picture book features a character named Al Foxword. Al is a high-pressure salesperson who will do anything to sell you the book he is featured in. Assume this character's persona throughout the program. Wear a bow tie like Al does. Be very energetic as you present each book and activity and also with your "patter" throughout.

Opening Picture Book

Watt, Mélanie. *Have I Got a Book for You.* Kids Can, 2009.

Al Foxword has a special deal—the book that is being read. He tries every sales pitch he can think of to get the reader to buy the book. At the end, he warns, "You break it, you bought it," and we see that one of the endpapers has a "corner torn off."

Storytelling Tip: There are several chances to use props during this "sales pitch." At one point, Al states that if you buy "my book in the next ten seconds, I will throw in your very own, top-of-the-line . . . BOOK MARK!" Pause before "BOOK MARK" and then whip out a book mark. Other selling points include wearing the book as a hat (put the book on your head), using the book as a mat (actually stand on the book), using it as a door-stopper (walk over and place it between the door and the door frame), using it as a coaster (set a cup on the book), and hiding behind it (hold it in front of your face).

Rap

"The Rappin' Rob Rap (Version 3)" by Rob Reid.

This rap is an updated version of "The Rappin' Rob Rap." Versions 1 and 2 can be found in *Something Funny Happened at the Library* (ALA Editions, 2003). For this particular program, I "become" Al from the Mélanie Watt book. Set up the rap in Al's voice, and state that he has other books to sell. "Sit right back and listen to THIS!" You can also use your own name in any of my raps. I know one young woman who starts out, "I'm Rappin' Sue and you know what I'll do; I'll tell you kids about books." I also know one young man who says, "I'm a rappin' guy and I'll tell you why; I'm telling kids about books."

> Well, I'm Rappin' Al and I'm your best pal, and
> I came to tell you 'bout books.

So lend me an ear; get over here! And don't give me no dirty looks.
I'm a storyteller, a pretty nice feller. There's no need for you to be wary.
Get your act together, get light as a feather, and fly down to the library.

We g-g-got . . . We g-g-got . . . We g-g-got . . . B-B-B-B-B-Books on . . .
We g-g-got . . . We g-g-got . . . We got-got books-books on . . .
There's Gooney Bird Greene
And Mercy Watson's charm,
I hear Dooby Dooby Moo
At the old Punk Farm.

Look—moody Judy Moody
And Stink—her little bro,
Some rhyming dust bunnies,
Oh, no! I gotta go!

An interrupting chicken,
Fly Guy, go on, scat!
A dog named Ike LaRue
And that Bad Kitty cat.

Is a scaredy-cat squirrel
The best pet of all?
Or is it Knuffle Bunny,
Pssst—hear the zoo call.

Don't forget the graphic novels
Sticky Burr and Babymouse,
The Lunch Lady's secret
Young Amelia rules this house!

There's that wimpy kid's book
Cave boys Ook and Gluk,
Watch out for Diaper Baby
And a flying psycho butt!

We g-g-g-got books!

Well, I've said my rap, now I'll take a nap,
Hope my dreams aren't scary.
'Cause when I wake up all new,
I'll find that my dreams have come true,
'Cause I'm going to the library!

Storytelling Tip: Have the following books or a sample title from the various series on display. As you read each line in the rap, point to each featured book and representative book from a series.

- The Gooney Bird Greene series by Lois Lowry
- The Mercy Watson series by Kate DiCamillo
- *Dooby Dooby Moo* by Doreen Cronin
- *Punk Farm* by Jarrett Krosoczka
- The Judy Moody series by Megan McDonald
- The Stink series by Megan McDonald
- *Rhyming Dust Bunnies* by Jan Thomas
- *Oh No, Gotta Go!* by Susan Middleton Elya
- *Interrupting Chicken* by David Ezra Stein
- The Fly Guy series by Tedd Arnold
- The Dear Mrs. LaRue/Ike LaRue series by Mark Teague
- *Bad Kitty* by Nick Bruel
- The Scaredy Squirrel series by Mélanie Watt
- *The Best Pet of All* by David LaRochelle
- The Knuffle Bunny series by Mo Willems
- *Pssst!* by Adam Rex
- The Sticky Burr series by John Lechner
- The Babymouse series by Jennifer L. Holm
- The Lunch Lady series by Jarrett Krosoczka
- The Amelia Rules series by Jimmy Gownley
- The Diary of a Wimpy Kid series by Jeff Kinney
- *The Adventures of Ook and Gluk, Kung-Fu Cavemen from the Future* by Dav Pilkey
- The Super Diaper Baby series by Dav Pilkey
- *The Day My Butt Went Psycho* by Andy Griffiths

Picture Book

Knudsen, Michelle. *Library Lion.*
Illustrated by Kevin Hawkes. Candlewick, 2006.

A lion walks into the public library. Everyone is nervous except for the head librarian, Miss Merriweather. "'Is he breaking any rules?' asked Miss Merriweather. She was very particular about rule breaking. 'Well, no,' said Mr. McBee. 'Not really.' 'Then leave him be.'" The lion sits in on story hour, dusts the encyclopedias with his tail, and licks the overdue notice envelopes. He brings help when Miss Merriweather falls and breaks her arm, but he leaves the library when told he broke a rule. We learn in the end, "Sometimes there was a good reason to break the rules. Even in the library."

Storytelling Tip: As Al, set up the selection by stating that Al likes to stay knowledgeable about the good books out there, so he is a frequent visitor to the library. And he has met many librarians in his day. This picture book is about a librarian who has an unusual visitor to her library. Later, in the story, when the lion roars, ask your audience to roar with him.

Chapter Book Selection

Colfer, Eoin. "The Test," from *The Legend of Spud Murphy.*
Hyperion, 2004.

As Al, state that some librarians are tougher than others and that the toughest librarian you ever met was nicknamed Spud Murphy. Legend has it that, when kids were noisy, she shot potatoes at them out of a gas-powered spud gun she kept under her desk. In this chapter, two brothers—Will and Marty Woodman—have been dropped off at the library by their mother. Spud has warned the brothers to stay in the library's junior section and not move from the carpet. When Marty decides to rearrange all of the books, Spud nails him with a book stamp. "She had appeared without a sound, like a ninja librarian." It takes him two hours to finish putting the books back in order. Marty is impressed by his adversary. He asks her to stamp his arm with her pirate flag stamp. She warns him the ink won't come off for a few weeks. Marty is horrified when he learns that, instead of a pirate flag, Spud branded him with the "I LOVE BARBIE" stamp.

Picture Book

Stein, David Ezra. *Interrupting Chicken.* Candlewick, 2010.

A young chicken constantly interrupts her father as he tries to read her bedtime stories. She warns Hansel and Gretel not to go to the house made of candy. "Don't go in! She's a witch!" She next interrupts by telling Little Red Riding Hood not to talk to strangers. She also tells Chicken Little not to panic. "It was just an acorn." Little Chicken writes her own story and starts to read it to her father. Unfortunately, he interrupts her with his snoring.

Storytelling Tip: As Al, tell the kids that you are seriously thinking of selling this next book because it is so funny. As you're reading the story, make your voice loud and excited when Little Chicken interrupts her father.

Joke

"A Chicken Walks into a Library," traditional, adapted by Rob Reid.

This library joke has been around for years. This is the version I developed. It's a slightly more elaborate version, and I put myself in the story. It rarely gets a big, direct laugh from the kids (it does get one from the adults), but after they think about it, I usually get a snicker or two. Usually some kids ask, "Did that really happen?" or state the obvious: "Frogs don't talk!" As Al, tell the kids that the *Interrupting Chicken* book "reminded me of the time I actually worked in a library. I still remember my weirdest day at the library . . ."

> I was working at the desk, when I looked up and noticed that a chicken had walked into the library. It walked straight up to me, looked me in the eye, and went "Bawk!" Well, I don't know about you, but to me, it sounded like the chicken said "Book!" So, I grabbed a picture book—I think it was *Chickerella*, by Mary Jane Auch—and tucked it under the chicken's wing. The chicken left the library. A short time later, the chicken was back. It walked up to me, dropped the picture book, and said "Bawk!" I determined the chicken wanted another book. Perhaps a chapter book. I grabbed a copy of *The Hoboken Chicken Emergency*, by Daniel Pinkwater, and stuck it under one of her wings. The chicken walked out of the library. About ten minutes later, it was back. The chicken walked

up to me, dropped the chapter book, and said "Bawk!" I assumed the chicken wanted yet another book. Perhaps a joke book this time, I thought. I grabbed *Why Did the Chicken Cross the Road?* by Joanna Cole, and tucked it under her wing. The chicken left the library. This time, I decided to follow the chicken. The chicken walked around to the back of the library, down a hill, and to a little stream. There, on the banks of the stream, was a frog. The chicken held up the book in front of the frog. The frog leaned forward to get a good look at the book. Then, it leaned back and said in a very loud froggy voice, "Read-dit!"

And that's what happened on my weirdest day as a librarian.

Storytelling Tip: Be sure to pronounce the frog's line as "Red-it" and not "Reed-it."

Readers' Theater

O'Malley, Kevin. *Once upon a Motorcycle Dude.*
Illustrated by Kevin O'Malley, Carol Heyer, and Scott Goto. Walker, 2005.

A girl and a boy are supposed to report on their favorite fairy tale for a library project. They can't find one they like, so they make one up. They disagree on various aspects of the story. The girl tells about a young princess named Princess Tenderheart. The boy wants the main character to be "a cool muscle dude" on a motorcycle. The two make several side comments about one another's story contributions. At the end, the princess and the dude get married and have a baby. Of course, the two storytellers can't agree if the baby is a girl or a boy.

Storytelling Tip: Have Al explain to the audience that some stories are fun to tell with more than one person. Ask a coworker of the opposite gender to read one of the two roles in the story. Your script for two readers can simply be the author's words.

Game

"Folklore Charades," traditional, adapted by Rob Reid.

Have the children take turns going outside of the story area, where they can't hear what's going on inside. Let two or three children go out together. It helps to have a second adult take them out and bring them back. Give the title of a well-known folktale to the remainder of the audience, and ask them how they might give visual clues about the folktale without talking; in other words, how could they mime the story so the other children can guess what it is?

For example, with the story "Chicken Little," one child can pretend she got bonked on the head by rubbing it, with a hurt look on her face. The child can then run in a circle waving her arms. Have her go up to a second child and point to the sky, and both children can run in a circle waving their arms. Add other children to this charade until someone guesses the story. If nobody guesses the story, have all the children who acted it out shout the story title together. Send three more children out, and plan miming the next story with the remaining children.

Here are some other folktales that can easily be acted out without words, along with a few suggestions to get things started:

- "Goldilocks and the Three Bears" (Mime eating porridge that's too hot.)
- "Hansel and Gretel" (Mime opening a door, the doorknob breaking off, and eating it.)
- "Jack and the Beanstalk" (Mime climbing up the beanstalk.)
- "Little Red Riding Hood" (Mime pointing and then making wide eyes with hand circles.)
- "Rapunzel" (Mime brushing extra-long hair, bundling it, and then throwing it out a window.)
- "Sleeping Beauty" (Mime pricking a finger and then rolling eyes into the back of one's head.)
- "The Three Pigs" (Mime huffing and puffing and blowing down a house.)

You can also play the game with nursery-rhyme characters such as Little Miss Muffet, Humpty Dumpty, and Jack and Jill.

Closing Picture Book

Perry, John. *The Book That Eats People.*
Illustrated by Mark Fearing. Tricycle Press, 2009.

The book in question is not a storybook or a dictionary. "It's a book that eats people." One time, it ate Sammy Ruskin of Little Rock, Arkansas. It also dispatched a library security guard and a little girl named Victoria Glassford. And now it's in your hands.

Storytelling Tip: After reading the last line, "And it eats people," pause and then SLAM the book shut.

Consider Substituting These Picture Books

Bottner, Barbara. *Miss Brooks Loves Books! (and I Don't).*
Illustrated by Michael Emberley. Knopf, 2010.

Miss Brooks is an energetic librarian who loves to dress up like book characters. Missy is not at all interested in books. She asks her mother if they could move. Her mother replies, "There's a librarian in every town." Finally, Missy finds the book just right for her: *Shrek!* by William Steig. She dresses up as Shrek and asks Miss Brooks to help her pass out stick-on warts for her classmates.

Storytelling Tip: When Missy has Miss Brooks distribute the stick-on warts, pass out commercially made stick-on green dots for your audience members to wear. Have them snort along with Missy when she pretends to be Shrek.

Child, Lauren. *Who's Afraid of the Big Bad Book?* **Hyperion, 2002.**

Herb falls into his collection of fairy tales and has many encounters with the characters. Goldilocks is upset because Herb is drawing attention away from her. "In case you pea brains have forgotten, this story is called 'Goldilocks and the Three Bears,' not 'The Little Show-Off in Pajamas Has Breakfast!'" Herb also runs afoul of the queen (earlier he had drawn a mustache on her) and Cinderella's wicked stepmother. Cinderella's fairy godmother finally pops him out of the storybook. Herb draws a mousy brown wig on Goldilocks and adds a padlock to the bears' house. "It serves her right for being such a MEANY."

Storytelling Tip: Some of the text is upside down because Herb had torn out the wicked stepmother's part and "put it back upside down." Make a big deal (exasperated looks, deep breaths, etc.) out of trying to read the book upside down and right to left.

Conway, David. *The Great Nursery Rhyme Disaster.*
Illustrated by Melanie Williamson. Tiger Tales, 2008.

Little Miss Muffet is tired of her own nursery rhyme and seeks out a new one. She finds "Jack and Jill" to be too painful, and climbing up a clock for "Hickory Dickory Dock" is too embarrassing. When the dish from "Hey Diddle Diddle" takes exception to Miss Muffet's running off with the spoon, the entire set of nursery rhymes is upset. Mary is followed by the three blind mice instead of the lamb, and Old Mother Hubbard falls off of Humpty Dumpty's wall.

Storytelling Tip: Because Miss Muffet's name gets interjected into various nursery rhymes, ask your audience for volunteers to substitute their names in a similar fashion. Never use a child's name without his or her permission. I learned the hard way that children can become easily embarrassed this way, so I always start with my own name as an example: "Jack and Rob went up the hill / To fetch a pail of water / Jack fell down and broke his crown / And Rob came tumbling after." Or "Hey Diddle, Diddle / The cat and the fiddle / The cow jumped over the moon / The little dog laughed to see such fun / And Rob ran away with the spoon."

Gerstein, Mordicai. *A Book.* Roaring Brook, 2009.

A literary girl character lives in the book with her family. She questions her role—more specifically, "What is our story?" Each family member gives a different answer, with each one playing the central character. The girl goes on a quest with a goose. She learns that the blobby things overhead are actually "readers." The two look over several fairy tales, mysteries, *Alice in Wonderland,* pirate stories, historical fiction, and science fiction. In the end, the girl determines that she will be an author and write her own story.

Storytelling Tip: This is a good opportunity for more booktalking. After reading the picture book, share an age-appropriate title or two representing each category mentioned in the story. For example, for third- and fourth-graders, you can show *My Teacher Is an Alien,* by Bruce Coville, as well as *The Wonderful Flight to the Mushroom Planet,* by Eleanor Cameron, to represent silly science fiction. You can highlight *Soup,* by Robert Newton Peck, or *A Long Way from Chicago,* by Richard Peck, to represent humorous historical fiction.

9

NOISY NONSENSE

Program at a Glance

Opening Picture Book: *The Louds Move In* by Carolyn Crimi and Regan Dunnick

Picture Book: *That's Good! That's Bad! On Santa's Journey*
by Margery Cuyler and Michael Garland

Oral Story: "Why I'm Late for School" by Rob Reid

Picture Book: *Noah's Bark* by Stephen Krensky and Rogé

Movement Activity: "Rain Storm," traditional

Picture Book: *Mmm, Cookies!* by Robert Munsch and Michael Martchenko

Picture Book/Readers' Theater: *Who Is Melvin Bubble?* by Nick Bruel

Closing Game: "The Telephone Game," traditional

Opening Picture Book

Crimi, Carolyn. *The Louds Move In.*
Illustrated by Regan Dunnick. Marshall Cavendish, 2006.

"Things have always been quiet on Earmuffle Avenue . . . Then one day, the Loud family moved in, and everything changed." Their neighbors Miss Shushermush, Mr. Pitterpatter, and Miss Meekerton ask the Louds to be quiet. When the Louds go on vacation, their neighbors are at first overjoyed. But then, they begin to miss the noise.

Storytelling Tip: There are plenty of noisy sound effects throughout the book for the audience to make. Create a sign for each sound effect and have an assistant hold each sign up at the proper time in the story as cue cards for the audience. The sound effects include the following words:

> Stomp stompity stomp
> Chomp chompity chomp
> WAAAAH!
> Bang bangity bang
> Thump thumpity thump
> Clack clackity clack
> HA HA HA
> CHA CHA CHA
> LA LA LA
> Hee hee hee
> Slam slammity slam
> Tee hee hee
> BURP!

Picture Book

Cuyler, Margery. *That's Good! That's Bad! On Santa's Journey.*
Illustrated by Michael Garland. Holt, 2009.

This is the third book in Cuyler's series, based on old skit routines. Santa Claus sets off on Christmas Eve to deliver toys. That's good. However, bad weather forces Santa's sleigh down by an igloo. "That's bad." But then we learn that "No, that's good!" They wait out the storm and leave some presents on the igloo. The rest of Santa's evening goes in the same pattern. Cuyler's other two books are *That's Good! That's Bad!* (Holt, 1991) and *That's Good! That's Bad! In the Grand Canyon* (Holt, 2002).

Storytelling Tip: Cue the audience that every time they hear you read, "Oh, that's good," their response in unison should be, "No, that's bad!" Conversely, every time you read, "Oh, that's bad," they respond by saying, "No, that's good!" There are fifteen such interactions throughout the story, with the last response reading, "Oh, that's good! No, that's TERRIFIC!"

Oral Story

"Why I'm Late for School" by Rob Reid.

I got the idea for this story from Garrison Keillor's sound-effects skits on his radio show, *A Prairie Home Companion.* Keillor typically tells an outlandish story, while his sound-effects guy adds his contributions. I tell my audience to make any sound effects they can think of to help the story. I often pause for them to insert these noises. Listed below is the script with the sound effects I normally get from the kids.

> The reason why I'm late for school? Oh yes, I have a very good reason.
> I was wearing my brand-new sneakers today. They
>   were very squeaky. ("Squeak-squeak.")
> I jumped into a puddle and my sneakers got squishy. ("Squish-squish.")
> They were squeaky AND squishy. ("Squeak-squeak, squish-squish.")
> I took off one shoe and blew on it to dry it off. (*Make blowing noises.*)
> A big bird swooped by and took my shoe. ("Hey!")
> I think it was a crow. ("Caw!")
> It could have been an eagle. ("Screech!")
> Or a parrot. ("Polly wants a cracker!")
> Maybe it was an owl. ("Hoot-hoot!")
> Or a rooster. ("Cock-a-doodle-doo!")
> No, roosters don't fly. It was definitely a crow. ("Caw!")
> I started running after the crow. (*Make drumming noises on the floor.*)
> I was running out of breath. (*Pant.*)
> I saw a tricycle and took it. It had one of those
>   little bells on it. ("Ding-ding!")
> It was too slow. I saw a motorcycle and took it. ("Vroom!")
> It was too slow. I saw a police car and took it. ("Whoo-eee! Whoo-eee!")
> The crow flew into the zoo. I followed. We went past
>   the monkey cage. ("Ooh-ooh! Aah-aah!")
> We went past the hyena cage. ("Ha-ha-ha-ha-ha!")

We went past the tiger cage. ("Roar!")

We went past the giraffe cage. (*Silence. Good for a big laugh.*)

We left the zoo. It was getting dark. I heard crickets. ("Chirp-chirp!")

I heard frogs. ("Ribbit-ribbit!")

I heard ghosts! ("Whooooo-oooo!")

It was still morning. A dark cloud had covered the sun. It
    started to rain. (*Cue the kids to snap their fingers.*)

It rained harder. (*Cue the kids again—slap legs.*)

I heard thunder. ("Boom!")

I started to cry. ("Wa-ah!")

The crow flew higher and higher. I had an idea. I
    chewed bubble-gum. ("Chew-chew.")

Lots and lots of bubble-gum. ("Chew-chew.")

I blew a big bubble. (*Make blowing noise.*)

I went up into the sky. ("Yow!")

I grabbed my sneaker from the crow. ("Got it!")

The crow popped my bubble. ("Pop!")

I fell down, down, down. ("No-o-o!")

Luckily, I landed on the school's trampoline. ("Boing!")

I ran to class. (*Pant.*)

And that's why I'm late for school!

If you don't believe that was a true story, just sit there quietly.

If you believe it *was* true, clap your hands!

Picture Book

Krensky, Stephen. *Noah's Bark*. Illustrated by Rogé. Carolrhoda, 2010.

In the old days, animals made whatever sounds came into their heads. The elephants sometimes went "cock-a-doodle-dooooo," the foxes went "quack quack," and the pigs howled at the moon. Noah was building an ark, and he had trouble concentrating. "'I NEED QUIET!' he barked." When it started to rain, some of the animals climbed into the ark. The crowded animals were "trying to keep their pointy parts to themselves." Noah made a lottery for animal noises, and those are the proper noises we know today.

Storytelling Tip: The audience members will quickly pick up which animal sounds to make when they hear them in the text. To simulate the lottery process Noah uses, divide the audience into six groups and hand each group a slip of paper. The papers have the following animal noises: "Hoooowwwllll," "Moooooowwww," "Bah-bah," "Oink," "Squawk," and "Roar." The text will clue each group when to deliver their sounds.

Movement Activity

"Rain Storm," traditional.

This traditional camp activity can be used to simulate the rain Noah and the animals faced. It's a longer version of the "rain" section from the "Why I'm Late for School" oral story, above. Direct the audience to rub their hands together to simulate a soft rain. After a few seconds of that, have them snap their fingers as the rain gets heavier. To make louder and louder rain, they should slap their legs louder and louder. Next, add a few thunder claps with voices. After a few moments of the loud noise, direct the kids to slap quieter and quieter to simulate that the storm is starting to pass. Switch over to finger snapping, and finally switch back to rubbing their hands. Tell them to give themselves "a round of applause" when the "rain" has passed.

Picture Book

Munsch, Robert. *Mmm, Cookies!*
Illustrated by Michael Martchenko. Scholastic, 2000.

Christopher sees a pile of play clay in the basement. He makes a pretend cookie and gives it to his mother. She takes a bite, makes a lot of noise, and has to brush her teeth. Christopher makes another clay cookie and gives it to his father. His father has the same noisy reaction. His parents notify Christopher's teacher. She makes a large clay cookie at school. Christopher takes a big bite of it, spits it out, and brushes his teeth. He learns his lesson and makes a real cookie for his parents, although the last picture shows them recoiling from it.

Storytelling Tip: The kids will automatically imitate the sounds in the text. As Christopher makes each cookie, he does it with a "whap, whap, whap"; a "swish, swish, swish"; a "chik, chik, chik"; a "glick, glick, glick"; and a "plunk, plunk, plunk." The kids will have the most fun making the gagging and spitting noises the characters make after they have tasted the clay cookies as well as the vigorous tooth-brushing noises.

Picture Book/Readers' Theater

Bruel, Nick. *Who Is Melvin Bubble?* Roaring Brook, 2006.

A variety of characters give their opinions about a young boy named Melvin Bubble in order for the reader to have a good idea about what he's like. Of course, we hear from his father (Melvin is just like him) and his mother (Melvin is the messiest boy in the world). We also hear from his best friend, Jimmy, who is impressed that Melvin can "whistle 'The Itsy-Bitsy Spider' through his nose!" But then things get weird. We hear about him from his dog (who basically barks the whole narrative), his teddy bear, the monster in his closet, Santa Claus, the Tooth Fairy, a beautiful princess (who is clearly thinking about someone else), the meanest man in the world, a magic rock, and a talking zebra.

Storytelling Tip: This is a great book to transform into a readers' theater production. If your audience is old enough, you can cast them as the different readers. If you don't have enough audience members, they can double up on roles. If your audience can't handle the readings, or you would prefer them to watch a more polished production, enlist several coworkers or community members to read the different roles. Including the narrator and Melvin, there are thirteen speaking parts.

Closing Game

"The Telephone Game," traditional.

Have the audience members get into a circle. If you have a large audience, make two or three circles. Explain the rules of this popular party game. The leader will show the phrase on a piece of paper to the first person in the circle. That person must then whisper the phrase to the next person. The message goes around the entire circle. The last person says the phrase out loud. The first person reads what is written on the piece of paper aloud so everyone can compare how much the phrase has changed. In most cases, the original phrase has been transformed into an entirely new and often nonsensical phrase. The rules are strict in regard to nobody repeating what he or she whispered. Perform this game several times, starting with different members of the circle each time. Think of some library- and literature-related phrases to start each game. Here are some suggestions:

> "The library is a cool place to hang out."
> "Where are the Captain Underpants books?"

"Do you know what happens at the end of Harry Potter?"

"Dr. Seuss tickles my funny bone."

"Who do you like better—Junie B. Jones or Judy Moody?"

Consider Substituting These Picture Books

Brett, Jan. *Honey . . . Honey . . . Lion!* **Putnam, 2005.**

The bird known as the honeyguide and the badger are "partners when it comes to honey." The bird leads the badger to the beehive, the badger rips it open, and the two share the honey. One day, the badger doesn't share, so the honeyguide decides to teach him a lesson. She guides him right into a bush where a lion is resting. The lion chases the badger all the way back to the badger's burrow.

Storytelling Tip: The story line is set up like the traditional story "We're Going on a Bear Hunt." There are several sound effects written into the text that the children can make. They will automatically make several hand gestures at various parts of the journey, too. These include splish-splashing through the water hole and swish-swishing "through a field of golden bristle grass." This is a wonderful technique for teaching kids about different habitats. You might want to do a follow-up activity where they study and make up a similar story set in a different region of the world. Be sure the animals and flora are specific to the new location.

Cordell, Matthew. *Trouble Gum.* **Feiwel and Friends, 2009.**

Ruben is a young pig stuck indoors on a rainy day. He's too noisy for his family, so Grammy gives him a piece of gum. "You know the rules . . . Don't swallow your gum. Don't play with your gum. And don't blow big, sticky bubbles with your gum." Of course, Ruben does all of those things with his gum.

Storytelling Tip: It's surprising how many sound effects one can come up with regarding bubble gum. Ruben chews it, gulps it, stretches it, snaps it, and, of course, pops it. The audience will have particular fun imitating Ruben when he chews in "super-slow motion" and then in "full-tilt, fast motion." There are other sound effects sprinkled throughout the text as well. This title would also work well with the "Naughty or Nice" lesson plan.

Fore, S. J. *Read to Tiger.* **Illustrated by R. W. Alley. Viking, 2010.**

A little boy is trying to read his book on the couch, but he's distracted by the sounds his tiger makes. First, the tiger chomps on bubble gum behind the couch. Next, the tiger is dressed up like a bear and growling. The tiger goes on to practice his karate moves and ride a toy train. The boy is finally fed up when the couch is lifted overhead with creaking noises. The tiger is looking for his whistle. The tiger finally quiets down and joins the boy on the couch to read a book featuring a tiger.

Storytelling Tip: The kids can join in with the tiger's sound effects. These include chomping the gum, growling like a bear, making karate noises ("Hi-ya!"), going "Choo-choo" and "Toot-toot," and making a "Creak-creak" sound when the couch is lifted.

Root, Phyllis. *Creak! Said the Bed.* Illustrated by Regan Dunnick. Candlewick, 2010.

When little Evie opens her parents' bedroom door, it goes "squeak." Evie is afraid and wants to sleep in her parents' bed. Her father snores, and her mother says, "Sure!" This begins a procession of family members joining them. Ivy is freezing, Mo is afraid, and even Fred the dog wants in. Poppa, who has been delivering a variety of snoring sounds, sits up and states, "There's no more room for Fred in the bed!" Fred jumps on board anyway, and the bed breaks, with a "crack." The book ends with everyone asleep and the floor making creaking noises as cracks start to appear.

Storytelling Tip: The kids can help make the sound of the door "squeaking" and the sound of the bed "creaking." Invert the text so that instead of reading, "Squeak, went the door," it now reads, "The door went squeak." This adjustment will help cue the kids to make their noises. Because the father makes a different snoring noise each time, it's funny to hold up cue cards for his sounds. His noises are "Snore," "Snark," "Snurkle," "Stop! There's no more room for Fred in the bed!" The audience members will also pick up on the extra thunder "Boom," Fred's "Woof," and the "Crack" when the bed breaks.

Smith, Cynthia Leitich. *Holler Loudly.* Illustrated by Barry Gott. Dutton, 2010.

"MAMA and DADDY LOUDLY named their baby Holler because he cried so loud." Everyone tries telling Holler to "HUSH," but it's no good. As he grows up, his loud voice disrupts school, the movie theater, fishing expeditions, the state fair, and the performance of the local barbershop quartet. Holler saves the day when his loud voice disperses a tornado heading to town.

Storytelling Tip: The author has provided several words in caps; read them louder than the rest of the text. At the end of the book, emphasize the "QUIET" capitalized words against the "LOUD" words. Cue the kids to yell "HUSH" with you when the townsfolk have had enough of Holler's loud voice. And feel free to let loose with your loudest voice of the day when Holler takes on the tornado.

10

PET SHOP

Program at a Glance

Opening Poem: "What's in a Name?" by Linda Ashman
from *Stella, Unleashed: Notes from the Doghouse*

Picture Book: *That Pesky Rat* by Lauren Child

Poem: "What Your Dog Might Be Thinking" by Karma Wilson
from *What's the Weather Inside?*

Picture Book: *The Birthday Pet* by Ellen Javernick and Kevin O'Malley

Musical Activity: "How Much Is That Turtle in the Window?"
traditional, with new words by Rob Reid

Poems: "What Your Cat Might Be Thinking" and "What Your Hamster
Might Be Thinking" by Karma Wilson from *What's the Weather Inside?*

Picture Book: *Billy Twitters and His Blue Whale Problem*
by Mac Barnett and Adam Rex

Musical Activity: "W-H-A-L-E," traditional, with new words by Rob Reid

Poem/Movement Activity: "At the Dog Park" by Linda Ashman
from *Stella, Unleashed: Notes from the Doghouse*

Picture Book: *Children Make Terrible Pets* by Peter Brown

Closing Poem: "The Things I Love" by Linda Ashman
from *Stella, Unleashed: Notes from the Doghouse*

Setup

Have pictures of assorted pets ready to tack to a wall or felt board. As the children enter the story-program area, ask them if they have pets and, if so, what kind. As they name the different types of animals, post the pictures for all to see. If some children don't have pets, ask them what kind of animals they think make good pets. Potential pictures to have on hand include dogs, cats, rabbits, fish, guinea pigs, hamsters, gerbils, mice, rats, snakes, lizards, turtles, frogs, parrots, canaries, parakeets, potbelly pigs, and horses.

Opening Poem

Ashman, Linda. "What's in a Name?" from *Stella, Unleashed: Notes from the Doghouse*. Sterling, 2008.

A dog's owners try a variety of names. The dog doesn't respond to "Binky, Mitzie, Fluff, and Fritz," as well as many other names. She does, however, perk up at the name Stella.

Storytelling Tip: After the poem, ask the children to pretend that Stella is in the backyard and we need to call her in. Everyone yells, "Stella!" Movie buffs will get a kick out of reenacting Marlon Brando from *A Streetcar Named Desire,* and the kids will simply have fun shouting.

Picture Book

Child, Lauren. *That Pesky Rat.* Candlewick, 2002.

A city rat is friends with a variety of domestic pets. The rat learns about the advantages of being someone's pet: sitting on a feather cushion, hanging out, or doing puzzles with the owner. The pets inform the rat about the downsides of being a pet. These include taking baths, being bored when the owner is away, or dressing up in a hat and coat. "But I would do anything to be somebody's pet." The rat puts up a poster that says, "Brown rat looking for kindly owner with an interest in cheese." A local pet-store owner also helps out. Soon, the nearsighted Mr. Fortesque comes in and takes the rat, mistaking it for a *cat.* Neither the rat nor the pet-store owner corrects him.

Storytelling Tip: The rat has a lot of lines, so I read them quickly and with excitement. You know, like those people who talk and talk and talk to you but never give you a chance to say a word.

Poem

Wilson, Karma. "What Your Dog Might Be Thinking," from
***What's the Weather Inside?* Margaret K. McElderry, 2009.**

Dogs like to pee, eat smelly things, frolic in rotten things, drink from toilets, munch on garbage, and *then* give people kisses. "SLURP!"

Picture Book

Javernick, Ellen. *The Birthday Pet.*
Illustrated by Kevin O'Malley. Marshall Cavendish, 2009.

Danny wants a turtle for his birthday. His father gets him a dog instead. The dog is too much to handle, so Danny's mother gets him a kitten. It makes Danny sneeze, so his brother gets him a rat. The rat keeps Danny up at night, so his sister gets him a bird. It's quite nasty. Danny says, "Not one of you listened to anything I said!" Danny gets his turtle. The other family members keep the other pets. The illustrations are fun, with Danny wearing a cardboard box painted to resemble a turtle.

  Storytelling Tip: The author sets up a rhyme as a clue to which pet Danny's family is getting him. "'You don't want a pet that sits still like a log.' So he went out and got Danny a . . ." Pause and let your audience shout out "Dog!" before turning the page. Do the same with the kitten, rat, and bird.

Musical Activity

"How Much Is That Turtle in the Window?"
traditional, with new words by Rob Reid.

Remind the children how the rat from *That Pesky Rat* waited in the pet store for the right owner and how Danny from *The Birthday Pet* had to try out several pets before finding the right one. It's important to match the right pet with the right owner. Tell the children to pretend they are animals in a pet store and that they hope to attract the attention of the perfect owner. As you sing the new lyrics to "How Much Is That Doggie in the Window?" the children will pretend to be sitting in a pet-store window acting out the motions of each animal. Start with a turtle as a nice follow-up to *The Birthday Pet*.

How much is that turtle in the window?
The one with a shell and a tail.

How much is that turtle in the window?
I sure hope that turtle's for sale.

How much is that kitten in the window?
The one with the nice furry tail.
How much is that kitten in the window?
I sure hope that kitten's for sale.

How much is that bunny in the window?
The one with the cotton-ball tail.
How much is that bunny in the window?
I sure hope that bunny's for sale.

How much is that snake in the window?
The one with the long, long, long tail.
How much is that snake in the window?
I sure hope that snake is for sale.

Ask the children to name other pets they can act out. It shouldn't be too hard to develop a quick second-line verse associated with the word *tail*. I had one child who suggested we use *gecko*. The kids basically got down on all fours and stuck out their tongues as I sang a line about "the one with a detachable tail."

Poems

"What Your Cat Might Be Thinking" and "What Your Hamster Might Be Thinking" from *What's the Weather Inside?* by Karma Wilson.

Your cat is probably dreaming about being the center of the universe and that no one is as good as she is. The poem ends with a warning: "And if you bring a puppy home, / well, that's the end of you." Follow that poem with the hamster version. The hamster is simply thinking "run" over and over before realizing, "Must . . . escape . . . the . . . plastic . . . ball."

Picture Book

**Barnett, Mac. *Billy Twitters and His Blue Whale Problem*.
Illustrated by Adam Rex. Hyperion, 2009.**

When Billy doesn't do what his parents tell him to do, they have a blue whale delivered to the house. "That's not just any blue whale, Billy. That's *your* blue whale. And it's your responsibility to take him wherever you go." Billy learns his lesson the hard way by taking his whale to school, where, ironically, he's teased. "Hey, Twitters . . . that blue whale is the stupidest pet I've ever seen. Why didn't you get a cool animal, like a dinosaur or something?" That evening, he's forced to feed and clean his whale. It came with an owner's manual, complete with waxing instructions. Billy finally decides it's easier to live inside the whale than outside. In another nod to movie buffs, a Pinocchio puppet can be seen in the final illustration.

Storytelling Tip: Have fun with the different characters' dialogue. I have Billy's parents speak as if scolding, his teacher in an excited voice, the bully in a monotone, and the boat captain with a "Popeye the Sailor Man" vocal treatment.

Musical Activity

"W-H-A-L-E," traditional, with new words by Rob Reid.

Ask the children if they are familiar with the traditional song "B-I-N-G-O." Sing a few lines of it to them. One can find many videos and sound clips of the song on the Internet. Tell them that we have a new version to go along with the book we just read. For each verse, another letter from the word *whale* is dropped and replaced with the audience members' clapping.

> There was a boy, he had a chore,
> That chore it was a Whale-O,
> W-H-A-L-E, W-H-A-L-E, W-H-A-L-E,
> That chore it was a Whale-O.

> There was a boy, he had a chore,
> That chore it was a Whale-O,
> (*Clap*)-H-A-L-E, (*Clap*)-H-A-L-E, (*Clap*)-H-A-L-E,
> That chore it was a Whale-O.

There was a boy, he had a chore,
That chore it was a Whale-O,
(*Clap-clap*)-A-L-E, (*Clap-clap*)-A-L-E, (*Clap-clap*)-A-L-E,
That chore it was a Whale-O.

There was a boy, he had a chore,
That chore it was a Whale-O,
(*Clap-clap-clap*)-L-E, (*Clap-clap-clap*)-L-E, (*Clap-clap-clap*)-L-E,
That chore it was a Whale-O.

There was a boy, he had a chore,
That chore it was a Whale-O,
(*Clap-clap-clap-clap*)-E, (*Clap-clap-clap-clap*)-E,
  (*Clap-clap-clap-clap*)-E,
That chore it was a Whale-O.

There was a boy, he had a chore,
That chore it was a Whale-O,
(*Clap-clap-clap-clap-clap*), (*Clap-clap-clap-clap-clap*),
  (*Clap-clap-clap-clap-clap*),
That chore it was a Whale-O.

Poem/Movement Activity

"At the Dog Park" from *Stella, Unleashed: Notes from the Doghouse* by Linda Ashman.

Before you read the poem, tell your audience that you have a movement exercise for them and they have to pretend that they are the dog in the poem. The poem discusses all the things a dog does in the park. This includes sniffing, scratching, dancing, rolling around, digging, howling, and more. At the end of the poem, the dog states that she is exhausted. "Could you carry me back home?"

Picture Book

Brown, Peter. *Children Make Terrible Pets.* Little, Brown, 2010.

Lucy, a young bear, finds a human boy in the woods. It squeaks at her. "OH! MY! GOSH! You are the cutest critter in the WHOLE forest!" She brings the boy to her mother and asks if she can keep him. Her mother replies, "Children make terrible pets." Lucy successfully convinces her mother, and she and the boy play together, eat together, and nap together. There are problems. The boy ruins the furniture, refuses to use the kitty-litter box, and throws temper tantrums. Lucy is devastated when the boy goes missing. She follows his scent through the woods and sees that he's reunited with his human family. To Lucy's ears, they are all squeaking, too.

Storytelling Tip: It's fun to read Lucy's lines with a Valley Girl voice. Also, cue the children to "squeak" along with the boy. Tell them to squeak when you point to his bright-green word balloons in the pictures. Finally, put up a mirror on the wall next to the pictures of pets. Tell the children that after the next poem, they can take a look in the mirror and see if they would make good pets or terrible pets.

Closing Poem

"The Things I Love" from *Stella, Unleashed: Notes from the Doghouse* by Linda Ashman.

The final poem from Ashman's collection describes all of the things Stella the dog enjoys. These include belly rubs, squeaky toys, and treats. In fact, treats are mentioned often in the poem. The last line is "Oh! Did I mention treats?" Serve your audience treats that pets like rabbits and hamsters might eat, such as carrot and celery sticks. Gummy worms also work well as food for lizards and turtles. Use your imagination. I thought I'd be clever and theme-savvy one time and served the popular homemade puppy-chow snack with melted chocolate and powdered sugar—in the library. Not a good idea.

Consider Substituting These Picture Books

Bachelet, Gilles. *My Cat, the Silliest Cat in the World.* Abrams, 2006.

For some reason, the book's narrator has trouble recognizing that his so-called cat is really an elephant. Sometimes the elephant acts like a real cat, curling up on the sofa or running around the living room. Other times, the elephant doesn't quite get it right, such as landing on its feet after a fall. The narrator winds up wondering what his cat's breed actually is.

Storytelling Tip: Read the book with a very straight face. The kids will be hollering that "it isn't a cat!" Plug along like you believe it *is* a cat, just like the book's narrator.

Bluemle, Elizabeth. *My Father the Dog.*
Illustrated by Randy Cecil. Candlewick, 2006.

A girl is convinced that her father is really a dog. She states her evidence. He likes to scratch, nap, and fetch the newspaper.

Storytelling Tip: Have an adult male coworker or a dad volunteer to act out the role of the father in the book as you read it aloud. As the narrator presents the following evidence that her father is really a dog, the "actor" can mime the following: "starts the day with a good scratch"; fetches the newspaper; plays tug-of-war; lies around for hours; chases a ball; "when he toots, he looks around the room like someone else did it"; and even uses a tree for a "pit stop." We simply had our "dad" smile and wag his finger as if to say, "Nope; not gonna act out that one." The book ends with "Mom says we can keep him." At this point, the reader, if female, gives the actor a pat on the head or, if not, recruits a woman in the audience to do so.

French, Jackie. *Diary of a Wombat.*
Illustrated by Bruce Whatley. Clarion, 2002.

A wombat mentions it is a native of Australia. It likes to sleep and eat grass—over and over and over. When humans move nearby, the wombat decides grass is boring. It trains the humans to give it food, and if they are slow to do so, it chews a hole in their door, bangs on the garbage cans, digs in the garden, and knocks clothes off the clothesline. It finally decides that "humans are easily trained and make quite good pets."

Storytelling Tip: Because the story is told by the wombat, read the text with a slow, drawn-out voice.

Ireland, Karin. *Don't Take Your Snake for a Stroll.*
Illustrated by David Catrow. Harcourt, 2003.

The rhymed-verse text warns about potential pet disasters. Your snake might make "small children shriek" if you take it "out for a slither." If you take your skunk for an airplane ride, he might get scared, and "there could be a terrible stink." The illustrations show the other passengers parachuting. Other strange "pets" to get this treatment include a coyote, an elephant, a duck, and a 'gator. The narrative ends with "Leave all of the animals tucked in at home / And take only people with you."

Storytelling Tip: Make felt animals and place them on the felt board as you read each animal's four-line verse. The kids in the audience will most likely shout out, "That's not a pet!"

Roberton, Fiona. *Wanted: The Perfect Pet.* Putnam, 2009.

Henry wants a dog so badly that he pays for an advertisement in the classifieds of the *Daily Catastrophe*. Meanwhile, a lonely duck spots the ad, dresses like a dog, and shows up at the boy's front door. "'A Dog!' yelled Henry. 'Woof!' said the duck." They play although the duck has trouble catching balls and learning new tricks. When the dog costume falls off, Henry is stunned. Then he gives "the duck a nice hot bath and a cup of tea." He also does research on ducks and learns good things about them. Ducks don't get dog breath, "won't eat homework, chew shoes or furniture, *and* won't pee on the carpet." He calls the duck Spot. "'Quack,' said Spot."

Storytelling Tip: Use a duck puppet throughout the story. When the duck dresses like a dog, tie the cut-off end of a black sock around the puppet's bill. Add some cloth strips for ears. If you're ambitious enough, you can also add a tail and "dog feet" similar to how the duck dresses up in the illustrations.

PART **3**

THE FUNNIEST BOOKS IN YOUR LIBRARY

11

PICTURE BOOKS

**Alley, Zoë B. *There's a Wolf at the Door: Five Classic Tales.*
Illustrated by R. W. Alley. Roaring Brook, 2008.**

Ages 5–10. A wolf moves from one story to another in this collection of five traditional folktales. First he encounters the three pigs—Alan, Gordon, and Blake—and runs away from them when he fails to get into the brick house. The wolf also appears in versions of "Little Red Riding Hood," "The Wolf and the Seven Little Goslings," "The Boy Who Cried Wolf," and "The Wolf in Sheep's Clothing." By the end of the book, the wolf decides that his food should have less personality, and he considers becoming a vegetarian.

Fun Moments: In the story of "The Boy Who Cried Wolf," the sheep make hilarious asides about the young sheepherder, such as "What a mutton head" and "We all had such high hopes for him. Better than Little Bo Peep."

**Amato, Mary. *The Chicken of the Family.*
Illustrated by Delphine Durand. Putnam, 2008.**

Ages 4–7. Henrietta is the youngest of three human girls. Her older sisters always tease her. One day, they tell her that she's a chicken. "Mom got you from Barney's farm." When Henrietta wakes up the next day, she finds a chicken feather and an egg in her bedroom. "Her sisters were right. She really was a chicken." Henrietta walks down to Barney's farm and plays with the chickens. Her sisters come to retrieve her, but Henrietta informs them, "I like being a chicken. These chickens are nicer to me than you guys are."

Fun Moments: Take a look at the expressions on the faces of not only the chickens but the animals in the background, including the girls' dog, who is wearing some type of clothing. The girls themselves have goofy expressions.

Aylesworth, Jim. *The Tale of Tricky Fox: A New England Trickster Tale.* Illustrated by Barbara McClintock. Scholastic, 2001.

Ages 5–9. Tricky Fox develops a plan to trick a human out of a fat pig. His brother says he'll eat his hat if it works. Tricky Fox finds an elderly woman. He asks her to watch his sack but to not look into it. The woman looks into the sack anyway and finds only a log. When she falls asleep, the fox throws the log into the fire. The next morning, he looks in his sack and wonders what happened to his loaf of bread. The woman can't tell him there was no bread without giving up the fact she peeked into the sack. So she gives him a loaf of bread. The fox pulls a similar trick with another old woman. The third time he tries the trick, the lady places her bulldog in Fox's sack. "And because of what happened, every fox in the woods has been much more respectful of humans. . . . And because of what happened, you never, ever see one wearing a hat."

Fun Moments: Tricky Fox hadn't counted on one thing—the third lady was a teacher. "And Tricky Fox didn't know that teachers are not so easy to fool as regular humans are."

Bachelet, Gilles. *My Cat, the Silliest Cat in the World.* Abrams, 2006.

Ages 4–7. The narrator talks about his cat, including how he sleeps on the couch but has little bursts of energy running around the house. The illustrations show that the "cat" is really an elephant. Young readers will enjoy the notion of an elephant hiding in the washing machine, cleaning itself (sucking water from the toilet with his trunk and spraying itself), and using the litter box. The narrator also talks about how cats usually land on their feet after falling and concedes his cat doesn't. We see the elephant on its back, with a broken loft railing overhead. The book ends with the narrator unsuccessfully trying to figure out his cat's breed from a cat book. There is a companion book titled *When the Silliest Cat Was Small* (Abrams, 2007).

Fun Moments: The author is trying to paint portraits of his "cat" in the artistic style of Norman Rockwell. The finished portraits include a Picasso-like elephant painting as well as an elephant posing as *The Birth of Venus.*

Barnett, Mac. *Guess Again!* Illustrated by Adam Rex. Simon and Schuster, 2009.

Ages 4–8. What looks like a simple rhyming guessing game for little children turns into a series of fun and absurd setups. For example, the first rhyme has a silhouette of what looks like a bunny; the text has clues like carrots, teeth, and ears; and we anticipate the rhyme with *funny* will be *bunny*. However, when we turn the page, we find that the answer is instead "Grandpa Ned." No, his name doesn't rhyme, but his contortions correctly match the silhouette. Grandpa Ned shows up again, and when we finally anticipate "Ned," because the setup's rhyme is *bread*, we learn that the answer is "Grandpa Alan."

Fun Moments: We anticipate that the creature eating our cheese and hiding behind the hole in the wall is a mouse. After all, the rhyming word is *house*. When we turn the page, we find a very huge Viking within the house's walls.

Barton, Chris. *Shark vs. Train.* Illustrated by Tom Lichtenheld. Little, Brown, 2010.

Ages 3–7. A shark and an anthropomorphic train compete head-to-head in many silly situations. Sometimes a scenario gives the advantage to the shark, and sometimes it gives the advantage to the train. For instance, the train has the advantage running a lemonade stand because its cars hold plenty of lemonade. The shark serves his lemonade at the bottom of the ocean and says to a diver-customer, "Whaddaya mean, 'It's a little watery?'" The shark has the advantage when jumping off the high dive into a pool of water. Sometimes, neither has the upper hand; when they are playing hide-and-seek, you can see the hidden shark's fin sticking up as well as the smoke from the hidden train. In the end, we see two boys playing with a toy shark and a toy train.

Fun Moments: The train has the advantage at an amusement park. There is a long line of kids waiting to ride the train. No one is in line to go on the shark ride. In fact, there is a sign that reads, "You Must Be This Crazy to Go on This Ride," complete with a height indicator.

Bottner, Barbara. *Miss Brooks Loves Books! (and I Don't).* Illustrated by Michael Emberley. Knopf, 2010.

Ages 4–7. Miss Brooks, the school librarian, is superexcited about books. She dresses up as children's book characters, and "all year long . . . reads us books." Unfortunately, the narrator doesn't feel the same about books. She asks her mother if they can move. "My mother says there's a librarian in every town." The girl finally gets excited when she finds the book *Shrek!* by William Steig. She dresses up as "a stubborn, smelly, snorty ogre."

Fun Moments: Some of the characters Miss Brooks dresses up as include the Runaway Bunny, Babar the elephant, one of the Wild Things from *Where the Wild Things Are,* the caterpillar from *The Very Hungry Caterpillar,* a turkey for Thanksgiving, a groundhog for Groundhog's Day, Abe Lincoln, and more. She even wears a fake nose with a wart in support of the narrator's costume. Another great image is Miss Brooks filling the narrator's backpack with books. There are more than twenty books in it!

Bruel, Nick. *Bad Kitty.* Roaring Brook, 2005.

Ages 3–8. This ABC book goes through the alphabet, not once, not twice, but four times. The first time we see Bruel's trademark cat being offered healthy food, from "Asparagus" to "Zucchini." Bad Kitty is not happy and decides to be bad. She acts mean. She "Ate My Homework" to "Zeroed the Zinnias." Bad Kitty is then offered a weird litany of food, from "An Assortment of Anchovies" to "Zebra Ziti." Bad Kitty decides to be good, from she "Apologized to Grandma" (earlier, she bit Grandma) to lulling the baby to sleep, "Zzzzzzzz." Bad Kitty appears in another concept book (*Poor Puppy,* Roaring Brook, 2007) as well as a series of easy chapter books.

Fun Moments: Kitty leaves a nasty note when she "Quarrels" with the neighbors. The note reads, "Dear Neighbor, Meow Hiss Hiss Hiss Meow Meow Hiss Meow!"

Bryan, Sean. *A Bear and His Boy.* Illustrated by Tom Murphy. Arcade, 2007.

Ages 4–7. The third book in the series, which also includes *A Boy and His Bunny* (2005) and *A Girl and Her Gator* (2006), follows a bear who wakes up to find a boy on his back. The two go through a day's routine together with all things that rhyme with *back.* The boy's name is Zach, and they eat flapjacks, perform jumping jacks, try out the new kayak, and watch horses at the track. The boy convinces the bear that he must be more laid-back and not run around like a maniac. They stop to smell the lilacs.

Fun Moments: Read the jacket blurbs on this and Bryan's other two books. Hugh G. Claws exclaims he couldn't put it down. Grizz Lee Bear adds, "Did I like it? Does a bear poop in the woods?" The author bio also mentions that because this book is about an animal with a child on his back, it's totally different from his other books, which are about children with animals on their *heads.*

Cole, Brock. *Buttons.* Farrar Straus Giroux, 2000.

Ages 5–8. When an old man's buttons pop off his britches, his three daughters work to solve this problem. The eldest daughter decides to walk around until a rich man falls in love with her and asks for her hand in marriage. She plans to say, "No! I can never be yours! Not unless you first give me all of your buttons!" The second daughter joins the army disguised as a boy so she can wear a soldier's uniform, which has several buttons. "I shall be able to spare two or three for Father." The youngest daughter plans to run around outside, holding her apron to catch buttons as they fall out of the sky. Of course, things don't go as planned, but in the end, all three daughters get married, and Father gets his buttons.

Fun Moments: At the end of the book, we learn that the youngest daughter's husband has his trousers "tied up with a bit of string. He doesn't seem to have enough buttons."

Cox, Judy. *Don't Be Silly, Mrs. Millie!* Illustrated by Joe Mathieu. Marshall Cavendish, 2005.

Ages 5–7. A young teacher makes her class laugh with her silly announcements. She tells the students to hang up their goats, instead of their coats. Illustrator Mathieu shows several goats hanging by their horns in the cloakroom. Mrs. Millie also tells the children to get out their paper and penguins (pens), don't cut in lion (line) to get a drink, wash their hands with soap and walrus (water), and put on their bats and kittens (hats and mittens).

Fun Moments: The children respond with their own funny saying: "We wave goodbye as we get on the octopus" (bus).

Creech, Sharon. *A Fine, Fine School.* Illustrated by Harry Bliss. HarperCollins, 2001.

Ages 6–8. Principal Keene loves his students, his teachers, and, most of all, his school. He decides to extend school to Saturdays. He then adds Sundays. He also has school on the holidays. No one knows how to tell him that they don't want to go to school this much. It's not until he has everyone attend in the summer that young Tilly lets him know that they need a break now and then.

Fun Moments: The illustrations are a hoot. Take notice of Tilly's dog, Beans, whenever he appears. In one scene, Beans is wearing a baseball catcher's gear. Illustrator Bliss also scattered several little notes around. There's a banner in the school cafeteria that reads, "Why Not Study While You Chew?" One child is holding a book, titled *This Book Is Way Too Hard for You,* while a classmate's backpack has written on it, "How's my walking? 1-800-SAF-WALK."

Cronin, Doreen. *Diary of a Worm.* Illustrated by Harry Bliss. HarperCollins, 2003.

Ages 4–8. A young worm discusses the advantages and disadvantages of being a worm. One of the negative aspects of being a worm is not being able to chew gum.

One positive note is that worms never get into trouble for tracking mud into the house. Worm talks about his family and friends, including Spider, who has his own book, *Diary of a Spider* (HarperCollins, 2005). A third book in the series is *Diary of a Fly* (HarperCollins, 2007).

Fun Moments: Worm and his friends dance to "The Hokey Pokey." They put their heads in and their heads out. "You do the hokey pokey and you turn yourself about. That's all we could do." A few pages later, Worm teases his sister by stating that her "face will always look like her rear end."

Cronin, Doreen. *Dooby Dooby Moo.*
Illustrated by Betsy Lewin. Atheneum, 2006.

Ages 4–9. It was a close call between this book and *Duck for President* (Simon and Schuster, 2004), both titles from the series that began with *Click, Clack, Moo: Cows That Type* (Simon and Schuster, 2000). *Dooby Dooby Moo* finds the farm animals entering a talent show. The cows sing, "Twinkle, Twinkle, Little Star," and the sheep sing, "Home on the Range." The pigs were supposed to do an interpretive dance, but Duck fills in for them with his rendition of "Born to Be Wild."

Fun Moments: Cronin, a lawyer herself, sprinkles legal jargon throughout the book, something not usually found in a children's picture book. Adults will appreciate the humor behind this idea. For example, the talent show ad states the trampoline prize is in used condition and there's no warranty. The second prize item, a box of chalk, comes with an asterisk that states, "Actual amount awarded will be based on availability." Third prize is a Veggie Chop-O-Matic.

Cronin, Doreen. *Rescue Bunnies.*
Illustrated by Scott Menchin. HarperCollins, 2010.

Ages 4–8. Newbie is a beginner first-responder. She and her shift pick up a distress signal. A young giraffe is stuck in mud, and a pack of hyenas is on the horizon. When the rest of her crew members threaten to pull out before the hyenas arrive, Newbie leads everyone to make one final effort to free the poor giraffe. The text is full of classic movie lines. For example, one of the crew tells Newbie, "You can't handle the truth." At the end of the story, the chief tells Newbie, "Here's looking at you, kid." Cronin even sneaks in the corny bit where one bunny tells another, "Surely you can't be serious," to which the second bunny replies, "Don't call me Shirley."

Fun Moments: Newbie reassures the young giraffe that "nothing is going to hurt you tonight. Not on my watch." The giraffe replies, "You had me at hello."

Elya, Susan Middleton. *Oh No, Gotta Go!* Illustrated by G. Brian Karas. Putnam, 2003.

Ages 3–7. A little girl is in the car with Papá and Mamá when she says, "Where is un baño? ¿Dónde está?" The family frantically races around town while looking for a bathroom. "Hurry, Papá. ¡Más rápidamente!" They finally enter a blue "restaurante" only to find a long line waiting to get into the bathroom. The ladies in line give the girl and her mother permission to go ahead of them. "I went to the baño, came out with a sigh, and thanked the nice ladies who let me go by." The family eats and drinks (the little girl has a huge glass of "limonada") and heads home. The sequel is *Oh No, Gotta Go #2* (Putnam, 2007).

Fun Moments: Of course, a few minutes into their drive on the way back home, the girl asks, "Where is un baño? ¿Dónde está?"

Ernst, Lisa Campbell. *Goldilocks Returns.* Simon and Schuster, 2000.

Ages 4–8. Years after the original story, Goldilocks (now an old woman) is feeling guilty about her horrid behavior as a young girl. She goes to the bears' house to "set things right!" The bears are older, too. In fact, the young one, "though not a baby for some fifty years now, still went by the name Baby Bear." While they are out on a walk, waiting for their porridge to cool (some things never change), Goldilocks installs new locks on their door, replaces their porridge with Rutabaga Breakfast Bars and Tart-n-Tasty Celery Juice, and restores Baby Bear's broken chair (it had been remade into a rocking horse). The bears find Goldilocks sleeping on their bed. She wakes up, gives them a hug, and leaves in her truck. The bears are upset at the changes she made.

Fun Moments: At the very end of the story, the bears are about to go on their walk when they spy another little blonde girl. "'Stop her! She might eat our food! She might mess up our fancy things! She might break my chair!' Very slowly they all smiled. And then, turning around, the bears happily continued on their walk."

Falconer, Ian. *Olivia.* Atheneum, 2000.

Ages 3–8. Olivia is a lively little pig who "is *very* good at wearing people out." She dresses up, sings "40 Very Loud Songs," sees a Jackson Pollock painting at the museum and tries to duplicate it on a wall at her family's home, and builds not a sand castle, but a sand skyscraper. At the end of the day, she negotiates with her mother on the number of bedtime books to read. This is the first book in a series.

Fun Moments: This first Olivia book has my all-time favorite line in any children's picture book: When Olivia's mother tells her daughter, "You know, you really wear me out. But I love you anyway," Olivia responds with "I love you anyway too."

Gerstein, Mordicai. *A Book.* Roaring Brook, 2009.

Ages 5–9. A little girl and her family live inside a book. When the book is opened, they wake up. We see them eat breakfast before the father goes off to be a clown, the mother fights fires, and the brother grows up to be an astronaut. The little girl worries. "Everyone has a story but me. What's *my* story?" Several literary characters with funny word balloons attempt to help the girl. A witch tells her, "Taste my roof! Taste my door! You can even eat my floor!" Her cat says, "This is a historical novel and I love it! It's full of mice!" The girl eventually decides to become an author.

Fun Moments: A goose is telling the little girl about the readers. The girl asks, "What are . . . readers?" The goose tells her to look up. The girl sees us and cries, "EEEEEK! What's that huge . . . *blobby* thing that looks something like a face?"

Graves, Keith. *Chicken Big.* Chronicle, 2010.

Ages 5–9. A big, humongous chick is born to a very small hen. An acorn falls on a small chicken, who worries the sky is falling. The big chick calms the other chickens down by eating the acorn. The same thing happens the next day with a drop of rain. Again, the big chick stops the panic. Every time the big chick helps out, the other chickens guess the big chick must be something else. "Apparently, he is an umbrella." A fox steals several eggs, and the big chick once again saves the day when the fox believes the big chick is a hippopotamus.

Fun Moments: When the smallest chicken blurts out that the big chick must be an elephant, the narrator informs us, "She was not the sharpest beak in the flock."

Himmelman, John. *Chickens to the Rescue.* Holt, 2006.

Ages 3–8. Various members of the Greenstalk farm family have little mishaps. Farmer Greenstalk loses his watch down the well. Mrs. Greenstalk is too tired to make dinner. The dog eats Jeffrey Greenstalk's homework. The sheep get lost. In each case, several chickens come to the rescue in a variety of creative ways. The audience will have fun repeatedly chiming the title phrase at the top of their voices. "Chickens to the rescue!" A sequel, *Pigs to the Rescue* (Holt, 2010), covers the same territory.

Fun Moments: In the case of Farmer Greenstalk's watch, chickens don swimsuits, snorkels, and fishing gear to retrieve the watch.

Isaacs, Anne. *Dust Devil.* Illustrated by Paul Zelinsky. Schwartz and Wade, 2010.

Ages 5–10. Angelica "Angel" Longrider, the larger-than-life tall-tale character from Isaacs's book *Swamp Angel* (Dutton, 1994), is back and now living in Montana, "a country so sizeable that even Angel could fit in." She wrestles a dust storm that contains a giant horse—Dust Devil—and creates the Grand Canyon as she holds on for the ride. She also encounters Backward Bart and his Flying Desperadoes gang, who ride on giant mosquitoes. "A Montana mosquito can carry a heavy suitcase and two watermelons on each wing without sweating."

Fun Moments: Angel moves a mountain closer to her cabin to create shade so that the sun doesn't wake her too early. Her neighbors all want a mountain, too. When Angel sets a new mountain down, she says, "That's a beaut. . . . And to this day, every stand-alone peak in Montana is called a butte."

James, Simon. *Baby Brains.* Candlewick, 2004.

Ages 3–8. The smartest baby in the whole wide world goes to school, repairs a car, and works "as a doctor at the local hospital," all while still an infant. Some scientists ask Baby Brains if he'd like to go into outer space. While taking a space walk, the extraordinary baby wails, "I want my mommy!" Baby Brains goes back to being a baby, but on the weekends "he still likes to help out at the local hospital." This is the first book in the Baby Brains series.

Fun Moments: "That evening, Baby Brains spoke his first words . . . 'I'd like to go to school, tomorrow.'"

Jenkins, Emily. *That New Animal.* Illustrated by Pierre Pratt. Farrar Straus Giroux, 2005.

Ages 3–7. A new baby comes into a home. The two dogs—FudgeFudge and Marshmallow—do not like that "new animal smell." They are jealous because they are no longer the center of attention. They think about burying the new animal like a bone. They think about sleeping in the new animal's cradle. Marshmallow pees all over the carpet. However, when Grandpa comes, the dogs are very protective of the new animal and bark at Grandpa to stay away.

Fun Moments: The two dogs think about eating the new animal. "'We'd get in trouble,' says Marshmallow. 'Then we'll just bite it.' 'No.' 'Bite it a LITTLE bit?' 'No.'"

Keller, Laurie. *Arnie the Doughnut.* Holt, 2003.

Ages 4–8. Arnie is an excited doughnut. He loves the bakery and is thrilled when a man buys him. However, Arnie's horrified to learn that the man plans to eat him. Arnie introduces himself and learns that the man's name is Mr. Bing. The two of them come up with lists of things to do with Arnie besides eating him. They decide on letting Arnie become a pet doughnut-dog. "Rolling over? Look at me—I was MADE for rolling over!" The little comments by other characters—many of them doughnuts—add to the book's humor.

Fun Moments: One long john prefers to be called "Long Jonathan."

Keller, Laurie. *The Scrambled States of America Talent Show.* Holt, 2008.

Ages 6–10. The anthropomorphic states of the union that first appeared in Keller's *Scrambled States of America* (Holt, 1998) are back because New York wants to put on a talent show. The other states are excited, except Georgia, who has a case of stage fright. They practice solo and group performances. Minnesota saws South Dakota in half, and North Dakota is in on the trick. Take time to read the many mini dialogues throughout the pages. During intermission, Vermont tells us, "If you need to use the 'you-know-what,' now would be a good time."

Fun Moments: The end shows Georgia imagining everyone in his or her underwear, a trick she was given to help her overcome her stage fright.

Ketteman, Helen. *Armadillo Tattletale.* Illustrated by Keith Graves. Scholastic, 2000.

Ages 4–8. Long ago, Armadillo had large ears he used to spy on the other animals. He spread gossip full of misinformation and caused trouble. Every time one of the animals got mad at Armadillo, it would peck away at his ears. Today, Armadillo has tiny ears, which actually allow him to run faster. He kept tripping over his old ears. He uses speed to his own advantage, but he no longer overhears what the other animals are saying.

Fun Moments: When Blue Jay, Rattlesnake, and Toad are told untruths by Armadillo, they throw hissy fits. "SQUAAAAWK! SQUAAAAWK! AAAAWK!"

Kloske, Geoffrey. *Once Upon a Time, the End: Asleep in 60 Seconds.* Illustrated by Barry Blitt. Atheneum, 2005.

Ages 4–9. A father reads to his child at night. "But as he read, he started cutting little words here and there and the stories would go faster, and faster, and faster." We are treated to the shortened versions of such classics as "Chicken Little," "Goldilocks and the Bears," "The Little Red Hen," and "Sleeping Beauty." Some of the titles themselves get shortened, such as "The Two Little Pigs." Most stories end with some reference about going to sleep.

Fun Moments: The story of "Princess Pea" tells of the sensitive princess who couldn't sleep because of the pea under the mattress. The father ends the story with "And so she married the prince. Is there a pea under your bed? Then what's your excuse? Go to bed."

Krosoczka, Jarrett J. *Punk Farm*. Knopf, 2005.

Ages 4–8. When Farmer Joe goes to the house for the evening, some of his animals get ready to play rock and roll. Pig plays the guitar, Cow plays drums, Chicken plays keyboards, Goat plays bass, and Sheep sings lead vocal. The horses wear sunglasses, take tickets, and act as security. The band plays a rousing version of "Old MacDonald." The next day, Farmer Joe finds all of the farm animals exhausted and sleeping. The rock band Punk Farm returns in *Punk Farm on Tour* (Knopf, 2007).

Fun Moments: At the end of the concert, Sheep belts out, "Thank you, Wisconsin!"

LaRochelle, David. *The Best Pet of All*. Illustrated by Hanako Wakiyama. Dutton, 2004.

Ages 4–8. A boy tries to convince his mother that he should have a dog. She tells him dogs are too messy and loud. He next asks for a dragon. She's amused and says, "If you can find a dragon, you can keep it for a pet." He finds a dragon at the drugstore and brings it home. The dragon causes many problems at home. The mother is fed up. The boy informs his mother that dragons are afraid of dogs. She agrees that they need a dog. The boy puts up a "Dog Wanted" sign, and within moments, a dog appears.

Fun Moments: At the end of the book, we see the dragon giving a thumbs-up to the boy.

Lowell, Susan. *Dusty Locks and the Three Bears*. Illustrated by Randy Cecil. Holt, 2001.

Ages 4–9. The three grizzly bears go for a walk to let their red-hot beans cool. In the meantime, a dirty little girl who "hadn't had a bath for a month of Sundays," hence her name Dusty Locks, sneaks into the bears' cabin. She eats the cub's beans, busts his three-legged stool, and falls asleep on his bed. The bears come home and find the intruder, who then escapes out a window.

Fun Moments: The western-style dialogue makes this a fun choice for storytellers to learn. When the bear cub finds his broken chair, he exclaims, "And someone's been sitting in my chair, and smashed it all to flinders!" When the big grizzly is upset at Dusty Locks's damage, he yells, "'BEAN RUSTLER! CHAIR BUSTER!'"

McFarland, Lyn Rossiter. *Widget*. Illustrated by Jim McFarland. Farrar Straus Giroux, 2001.

Ages 3–8. Mrs. Diggs's cats, "the girls," don't like the new stray dog. However, he first confuses them and then wins them over by meowing, hissing, spitting, and growling. Widget starts barking when Mrs. Diggs has an accident. The surprised cats start barking, too, and help quickly arrives. The sequel is *Widget and the Puppy* (Farrar Straus Giroux, 2004).

Fun Moments: While Widget and "the girls" are sizing each other up, the six cats puff up, trying to intimidate the dog. Widget, in turn, puffs up back at them. Later, Widget uses the litter box.

McMullan, Kate. *I Stink!* Illustrated by Jim McMullan. HarperCollins, 2002.

Ages 3–8. An anthropomorphic garbage truck with an attitude talks directly to the reader. "Know what I do at night while you're asleep? Eat your trash, that's what." The truck is unapologetic if it wakes you up while collecting and compacting the garbage. Companion books include *I'm Mighty!* (HarperCollins, 2003), which follows a tugboat; *I'm Dirty!* (HarperCollins, 2006), which features a backhoe loader; *I'm Bad!* (HarperCollins, 2008); and *I'm Big!* (Balzer and Bray, 2010). The latter two both showcase dinosaurs.

Fun Moments: The middle section of the picture book is an alphabetical litany of trash items, such as "Apple cores, Banana peels, Candy wrappers"—all the way to "Zipped-up ziti with zucchini."

Monks, Lydia. *Aaaarrgghh! Spider!* Houghton Mifflin, 2004.

Ages 3–8. A spider wants to become a human family's pet. Unfortunately, whenever anyone spots her, they shout out "Aaaarrgghh! Spider!" Dad traps the spider and lets her go outside. She returns. She wants to prove to the humans that she's clean and appears in the bathtub. Mom flushes her down the drain. The kids in the audience will yell the title phrase with the book characters and then "ooh" and "aah" when they see the sparkly webs the spider weaves.

Fun Moments: There's a particularly silly picture of the spider on a leash going for a walk with the family.

Monroe, Chris. *Sneaky Sheep.* Carolrhoda, 2010.

Ages 3–8. Blossom and Rocky try to sneak out of their meadow to reach a yummy green patch way up high on a mountainside. Their watchdog, Murphy, is very good about keeping them where they belong. The two sheep see their chance to run away when Murphy is helping another sheep get her foot out of a gopher hole. Blossom and Rocky run into the woods. A wolf appears and tells the two sheep, "Don't hurry off! You just got here!" Murphy saves the day, and the two sheep learn their lesson—for a while.

Fun Moments: In addition to the zigzag trails the two sheep take to lose Murphy (and he always finds them), there is a double-page spread illustrating the point that "they had been known to make some bad decisions over the years." We see Blossom and Rocky skateboarding without helmets, playing poker with those famous poker dogs, running with scissors, and also running with the bulls.

O'Malley, Kevin. *Animal Crackers Fly the Coop.* Walker, 2010.

Ages 4–9. This remake of the traditional story "The Brementown Musicians" features a wisecracking Hen. "How do comedians like their eggs? Funny-side up!" She is joined by fellow comedians Dog, Cat, and Cow. They scare away some robbers, take over their house, and open a comedy club. Along with the animals' riddles—"Why didn't the skeleton cross the road? He didn't have the guts"—the narration is full of puns. "It didn't take much *purr*-suasion to get the cat to go with them."

Fun Moments: Watching my wife roll her eyes as I read the riddles out loud.

Palatini, Margie. *Bad Boys.* Illustrated by Henry Cole. HarperCollins, 2003.

Ages 4–9. Willy and Wally Wolf—the bad boys, as in "big bad wolves"—are running away from Little Red Riding Hood and the Three Little Pigs. They hide themselves in a flock of sheep—"two wolves in sheep's clothing"—with the intention of eating the sheep. Old Betty Mutton isn't fooled, however, and she arranges for the bad boys to get sheared by the farmers. The wolves reappear in *Bad Boys Get Cookie!* (Katherine Tegan, 2006) and *Bad Boys Get Henpecked!* (Katherine Tegan, 2009).

Fun Moments: One of the sheep is introduced as Meryl Sheep. There's also a hilarious picture of one of the wolves putting on pantyhose.

Palatini, Margie. *Lousy Rotten Stinkin' Grapes.*
Illustrated by Barry Moser. Simon and Schuster, 2009.

Ages 4–9. Fox spots some grapes high up on a vine growing on a tree. He enlists Bear, Beaver, Porcupine, and Possum to help him but doesn't listen to their suggestions. "You leave the thinking to me. After all, I'm the fox. Sly. Clever. Smart. I know how to get grapes." He eventually gives up. The final illustration shows the other animals enjoying the grapes they managed to bring down with little difficulty.

Fun Moments: Not only does Fox ignore the others' ideas, but he is also downright rude. He tells Porcupine not to get prickly and calls Beaver his "dentally challenged chum."

Plourde, Lynn. *School Picture Day.* Illustrated by Thor Wickstrom. Dutton, 2002.

Ages 5–8. All of the students get dressed up for school picture day, all except Josephina Caroleena Wattasheena the First. She'd rather learn how things work with her tool kit. She takes apart the school bus gearshift and, in the process, gets grease on the other kids. She takes apart a pencil sharpener, and her classmates get covered with wood shavings. She messes with the school's sprinkler system and soaks the class. After a few more similar episodes, Josephine saves the day by fixing the photographer's camera.

Fun Moments: To get the children to smile, the photographer has an array of humorous sayings. These include "Everyone, say cheesy weezy, if you pleasy" and "Teethy weethies, let's see those teethies." When Josephine fixes the camera, all she says is "Smile."

Pulver, Robin. *Author Day for Room 3T.*
Illustrated by Chuck Richards. Clarion, 2005.

Ages 5–9. Harry Bookman, the author of *The Banana from Outer Space, Ants in My Lunch Box,* and *The Mystery of the Missing Monkey Bars,* is coming to visit the students in Room 3T. They are excited but aren't exactly sure what he looks like. The images they conjure range from space traveler to superhero. A chimpanzee enters the class, and the children assume he is Harry Bookman. Their teacher has inconveniently lost her glasses, and she doesn't suspect anything's wrong.

Fun Moments: One teacher tells the class, "No monkey business." We see many of the children looking and behaving like monkeys.

Ransom, Jeanie Franz. *What Really Happened to Humpty?*
(From the Files of a Hard-Boiled Detective).
Illustrated by Stephen Axelsen. Charlesbridge, 2009.

Ages 5–10. When Humpty Dumpty falls off the wall, his brother Joe investigates. Joe works his way around Mother Gooseland, interviewing everyone from Goldilocks to Old Mother Hubbard. He learns a big wind occurred about the same time that both the Three Pigs' new house went down and Humpty took his spill. Joe Dumpty solves the case, which involves both the Big Bad Wolf and Muffy, aka Little Miss Muffet.

Fun Moments: When Joe finds Humpty on the ground, Muffy says, "At least he landed sunny-side up." Joe is so mad, he says, "Whoever did this [is] gonna fry." Mother Goose tells Joe that Humpty's fall was an accident. "There's no case to crack."

Rex, Adam. *Pssst!* Harcourt, 2007.

Ages 3–9. A girl is walking through the zoo when she hears the title sound, "Pssst!" A gorilla wants her to find him a new tire. His old tire swing broke. The girl says, "Well . . . I guess so." She moves on. She hears the noise again. A wild boar wants her to bring a trash can. And so on. The girl hears requests from bats, a hippo, penguins, sloths, turkeys, a baboon, a tortoise, and a peacock. "Luckily there was a store across the street that sold everything." The animals use the items to make their escape from the zoo.

Fun Moments: The background illustrations are full of wonderful images and signs. We see a small deer in one of those rolling hamster balls in one picture, and a few pages later, we see a rhino in another hamster ball.

Rex, Michael. *Furious George Goes Bananas.* **Putnam, 2010.**

Ages 5–10. In this parody of Curious George, Furious George is captured by a man in a funny hat. This man sells George first to a zookeeper, then to a construction foreman, next to a Broadway director, and, finally, to a rocket scientist. In the end, George gets his revenge against the man in the funny hat by tricking the man into going into outer space. Rex made two more parodies of classic picture books: *Goodnight Goon* (Putnam, 2008) is a retelling of *Goodnight Moon,* and *The Runaway Mummy* (Putnam, 2009) is a twist on *The Runaway Bunny.*

Fun Moments: The man in the funny hat keeps trying to pawn George off as a monkey. Each time, he is corrected by the other humans, who tell him monkeys have tails. George is an ape.

Schneider, Howie. *Chewy Louie.* **Rising Moon, 2000.**

Ages 3–7. Chewy Louie, the new pet puppy, eats everything in sight. After he eats his dog food, he eats the bowl. He also eats toys, the back porch, lumber on the back of a lumber truck, and a dog trainer's guitar.

Fun Moments: The dog finally grows up and apparently has stopped chewing everything in sight. Everyone seems to be happy. The reader then notices that one of the back endpapers has a big bite taken out of it.

Shannon, David. *Duck on a Bike.* **Scholastic, 2002.**

Ages 3–7. Duck finds a boy's bike and begins to ride it around the farm. The other farm animals react in different ways. The cat could care less, while the dog thinks, "It's a mighty neat trick." The chicken is startled, and the goat wants to eat the bike. When several kids ride to the farm and run inside the farmhouse, all of the farm animals have bright looks on their faces. Soon, they are all riding the bikes. At the end of the book, Duck is eyeing a tractor.

Fun Moments: When the goat gets on a bike, he starts eating the bike's basket. The chicken riding a tricycle is also worth the price of the book.

Sierra, Judy. *Tell the Truth, B.B. Wolf.* **Illustrated by J. Otto Seibold. Knopf, 2010.**

Ages 4–8. This sequel is even funnier than the first book to feature B.B. Wolf (*Mind Your Manners, B.B. Wolf,* Knopf, 2007). B.B. attempts to tell his side of the Three Pigs story, but he is shouted down by the pigs in the audience. He eventually apologizes and helps build the pigs their "very own piggyback mansion." There are some fun Tom Swifties in the text: "'No one is falling for your story,' cracked Humpty Dumpty."

Fun Moments: Adults, at least, will laugh when the wolf's cell phone goes off with a "Who's Afraid of the Big Bad Wolf" ringtone.

Smith, Lane. *It's a Book.* Roaring Brook, 2010.

Ages 4–10. A jackass asks a monkey about the item he's holding. The monkey replies, "It's a book." The jackass asks a series of questions about this book. "How do you scroll down?" "Does it need a password?" When the jackass asks, "Where's your mouse?" a tiny rodent appears from under the monkey's hat. Of course, the jackass becomes engrossed with the book, and the monkey decides to head for the library. At the end of the book, the mouse says a line few authors have the clout to get away with: "It's a book, Jackass."

Fun Moments: The monkey shows the jackass a page from the book *Treasure Island.* Long John Silver is pulling out his sword and laughing at Jim. Jim sees a ship in the distance and smiles. The jackass decides there are too many letters and "fixes" the text so that it now reads, "LJS: rrr! K? lol! JIM: :(! :)"

Smith, Lane. *John, Paul, George and Ben.* Hyperion, 2006.

Ages 5–10. Smith plays off the Beatles' names to teach us funny aspects about the Sons of Liberty: John Hancock, Paul Revere, George Washington, Ben Franklin, and Thomas Jefferson. They are all portrayed as children who had habits we associate with their grown-up lives. John Hancock filled an entire school chalkboard with his signature. Ben Franklin came up with so many "wise sayings that his acquaintances came up with one of their own—'Please shut up your big yap!'" Smith also includes a chart in the back of the book "wherein we set the record straight with ye olde Truth or False section."

Fun Moments: Paul Revere hollers while helping a woman at the store where he works. "EXTRA-LARGE UNDERWEAR? SURE WE HAVE SOME! LET'S SEE, LARGE . . . LARGE . . . EXTRA LARGE! HERE THEY ARE! GREAT, BIG, EXTRA-LARGE UNDERWEAR!"

Solheim, James. *Born Yesterday: The Diary of a Young Journalist.* Illustrated by Simon James. Philomel, 2010.

Ages 4–8. A newborn baby makes several observations about the world. The baby is fascinated by the big sister, who can play the harmonica, "an important life skill." The baby is impatient to grow up and go to school. After all, even the dog, Foofy, gets to go to a school. After worrying about his (or her) relationship with the big sister, the baby is startled to hear her say that "you are my best friend. Baby then states, 'I was so relieved that I tried to eat her hair.'"

Fun Moments: The baby has an epiphany. "Finally—I have it figured out. Some things are noses, some are taxicabs, and some are Belgians."

Spinelli, Eileen. *Silly Tilly.* Illustrated by David Slonim. Marshall Cavendish, 2009.

Ages 3–7. Tilly is a fun-loving goose, "a daffy-down-and-dilly goose," who sometimes irritates the other farm animals with her antics. She tickles the frogs and sits on Rooster's birthday cake. She stops her antics until the other animals notice they haven't laughed in a long time. "It's dullsville on the farm. No fun!" They apologize to Tilly, and she goes back to her old ways.

Fun Moments: When the animals first yell at Tilly, she is wearing ancient Egyptian gear and "walking like an Egyptian."

Stein, David Ezra. *Interrupting Chicken.* Candlewick, 2010.

Ages 3–8. Papa begins reading a bedtime story to a little red chicken. She promises not to interrupt. However, once Papa starts reading "Hansel and Gretel," Little Chicken interrupts and shouts "Don't go in! She's a witch!" Papa switches stories and begins reading "Little Red Riding Hood." Little Chicken once again interrupts. "Don't talk to strangers!" She does it one more time, when Papa reads the story "Chicken Little." Papa is flabbergasted. Little Chicken begins reading Papa a story titled "Bedtime for Papa." Papa falls asleep.

Fun Moments: The characters in the stories also react to Little Chicken's interruptions. Hansel and Gretel are startled, as is the witch, who is wearing an apron that says "Kid Soup" on it. The Big Bad Wolf in "Little Red Riding Hood" falls down, and the various fowl in "Chicken Little" lose a feather or two.

Teague, Mark. *Dear Mrs. LaRue: Letters from Obedience School.* Scholastic, 2002.

Ages 4–9. Ike LaRue, a dog, is sent to the Igor Brotweiler Canine Academy, an obedience school, by his owner, Gertrude LaRue. The dog sends a series of letters to his owner complaining about the terrible conditions. Black-and-white illustrations prove his point. Accompanying color pictures, however, show that his real surroundings are posh and wonderful. This is the first book in a series.

Fun Moments: One example shows a black-and-white image of Ike begging for another bowl of gruel, á la Oliver Twist. In reality, his menu shows the Brotweiler specialty—a "golden chewy bone with gravy."

Thomas, Jan. *Rhyming Dust Bunnies.* Atheneum, 2009.

Ages 3–8. In what may be the silliest "scratch-your-head-and-try-to-figure-out-where-this-idea-came-from" picture-book concept since Mo Willems's *Don't Let the Pigeon Drive the Bus!* we follow four colorful specks of dust playing rhyming games. Ed, Ned, Ted, and Bob talk directly to the reader. Ed, Ned, and Ted shout out words that rhyme, while Bob shouts out other words and phrases. We soon learn that Bob is warning the others about danger. The companion book is titled *Here Comes the Big, Mean Dust Bunny!* (Atheneum, 2009).

Fun Moments: When the other three "dust bunnies" rhyme *dog,* Bob blurts out, "Look out! Here comes a big scary monster with a broom!" The other characters say, "Bob, no . . . 'Look out! Here comes a big scary monster with a broom!' does not rhyme with *anything,* really."

**Vernick, Audrey. *Is Your Buffalo Ready for Kindergarten?*
Illustrated by Daniel Jennewein. Balzer and Bray, 2010.**

Ages 5–7. A little girl brings her buffalo, complete with a backpack, to kindergarten with her. As the young readers read about the buffalo, they also learn some basic rules of kindergarten, such as "cooperating" and "taking turns."

Fun Moments: The buffalo learns to share, but the other kids balk at snack time when the buffalo pulls out grass. "But he may be the only one who eats grass, then throws it up in his mouth and eats it again. Remember: Everyone's special in his or her own way."

Watt, Mélanie. *Scaredy Squirrel.* Kids Can Press, 2006.

Ages 4–8. Scaredy Squirrel is afraid of leaving his tree. He's also afraid of "tarantulas, poison ivy, green Martians, killer bees, germs, and sharks." His daily routine is boring but safe. One day, he thinks a killer bee is after him and he jumps from his tree. It turns out that he's a flying squirrel, and he creates a "new-and-improved daily routine" that includes jumping into the unknown. This is the first book in a series.

Fun Moments: Scaredy Squirrel's emergency kit includes a can of sardines to distract the sharks if they attack. The front endpapers include a warning from Scaredy Squirrel for the reader to "wash their hands with antibacterial soap before reading this book."

Why Did the Chicken Cross the Road? Dial, 2006.

Ages 4–10. Fourteen children's book illustrators try to explain the age-old question through their pictures. Marla Frazee's explanation is that a sunny, grand building awaits the chicken on the other side—and as the chicken is leaving behind a rainy, dreary, gray chicken shack, she is thinking "Duh." Chris Sheban shows a guilty-looking chicken holding a baseball bat looking at a broken window. Harry Bliss has the chicken escaping a horde of "mutated zombie chickens from Mars." Lynn Munsinger's answer is simple: "Because the light said 'Walk.'" The other illustrators are Jon Agee, Tedd Arnold, David Catrow, Mary GrandPré, Jerry Pinkney, Vladimir Radunsky, Chris Raschka, Judy Schachner, David Shannon, and Mo Willems.

Fun Moments: The back section contains a "Scoop from the Coop." The contributors respond to the question, "Why did the artist cross the road?"

Wilcox, Leah. *Falling for Rapunzel.* Illustrated by Lydia Monks. Putnam, 2003.

Ages 4–8. A prince tries to rescue Rapunzel from her tower. Unfortunately, she is hard of hearing. She mistakes his words and tosses down dirty socks (instead of "curly locks"), a cantaloupe (when he asks for "a rope"), and some pancake batter (instead of a "ladder"). When Rapunzel throws down her maid instead of her braid, the prince decides to ride off with the cute servant.

Fun Moments: When the prince cries, "Rapunzel, Rapunzel, throw down your hair," she thinks he said "underwear." A pair of pink panties lands on his head.

Willems, Mo. *Don't Let the Pigeon Drive the Bus!* Hyperion, 2003.

Ages 3–7. A bus driver asks the reader to "watch things for me until I get back. Thanks. Oh, and remember: Don't Let the Pigeon Drive the Bus!" Pretty soon, a pigeon comes along and asks to drive the bus. The pigeon doesn't take no for an answer and displays a variety of arguments and emotions to change the reader's mind. This is the first book in a series.

Fun Moments: The pigeon tries to influence the reader by stating, "I have dreams, you know!" right before it explodes into a frenzied "hissy-fit."

Willems, Mo. *Knuffle Bunny.* Hyperion, 2004.

Ages 3–7. Daddy takes Trixie to the Laundromat. They accidentally put her stuffed bunny, which Trixie calls Knuffle Bunny, into one of the washing machines. Outside of the Laundromat, Trixie realizes that Knuffle Bunny is no longer with them. She has trouble communicating this fact to her father. However, once her mother is on the scene, the adults quickly realize that Knuffle Bunny is missing. This is the first book in a series.

Fun Moments: At one point, Trixie fusses and goes "boneless" (her father has a hard time picking her up). In another picture, they run past a man wearing a T-shirt featuring the main character from Willems's *Don't Let the Pigeon Drive the Bus!*

12

EASY READERS

Arnold, Tedd. *Hi! Fly Guy.* Scholastic, 2005.

Ages 5–8. A boy catches a fly named Fly Guy for the Amazing Pet Show. The boy is astounded that the fly is able to say the boy's name—Buzz. "You are the smartest pet in the world!" The judges laugh and say, "Flies can't be pets. Flies are pests!" Fly Guy shows the judges some fancy flying tricks, says his owner's name, and performs a diving act into his own jar. They award Fly Guy with the "Smartest Pet" award. This is the first book in the Fly Guy series.

Fun Moments: Buzz and his parents feed Fly Guy by sticking an entire hot dog and bun in Fly Guy's jar.

Caple, Kathy. *Duck and Company.* Holiday House, 2007.

Ages 5–8. Rat and Duck run a bookstore. When Cat comes in looking for a cookbook, Rat hides. "I'm looking for a book that tells how to cook rats." Duck successfully convinces Cat that a book about carrots is much better. A humorless Badger wants to buy a joke book and doesn't laugh at anything until Duck accidentally falls into a garbage can. Duck also performs a very successful story hour for "a stampede of little mice, frogs, rats, bunnies, and turtles."

Fun Moments: While waiting for her chicks to hatch, Mother Hen turns down Duck's suggestion of the book *I Love You, My Dumplings* and instead buys a book titled *Terror Tales to Make Your Eyes Pop Out.*

Catrow, David. *Max Spaniel: Dinosaur Hunt.* **Orchard, 2009.**

Ages 5–8. Max the dog dons his pith helmet, grabs his butterfly net, and goes look-ing for dinosaurs in his backyard. "A great hunter knows where to look." He states that a football he found in the flower bed is really a dinosaur head. A toy fire truck is a dinosaur's knee, a garden hose is a neck, a hockey stick is a jaw, and a tricycle makes up a dino's hips. Max gathers more things and begins to assemble them, to the amusement of a cat. However, once all of the pieces are put together, "The dinosaur comes alive," and the cat takes off in horror.

Fun Moments: The dog places a flower over his own mouth to simulate the dino-saur's lips. The illustration is a cross between funny and creepy. This is the first book in the Max Spaniel series.

Griffiths, Andy. *The Cat on the Mat Is Flat.*
Illustrated by Terry Denton. Feiwel and Friends, 2006.

Ages 4–7. In the spirit of Dr. Seuss, Griffiths created nine silly stories heavy on simple phonics and end rhymes. We meet Ed, Ted, Ted's dog Fred, and a whale named Ned in one story. There's also Harry Black who carries his snack in a sack. The book's thick chapter-book format will appeal to kids facing reading challenges who are slightly older than the typical easy-reader audience. The companion book is *The Big Fat Cow That Goes Kapow* (Feiwel and Friends, 2009).

Fun Moments: Read the chapter titled "Duck in a Truck in the Muck," which features a duck named Chuck. Chuck gets his ice-cream truck stuck in the muck. "What bad luck." Buck shows up with his "brand-new shiny muck-sucking truck." Unfortunately, Buck's truck sucks up Buck and Chuck as well as Chuck's truck.

McMullan, Kate. *Pearl and Wagner: Two Good Friends.*
Illustrated by R. W. Alley. Dial, 2003.

Ages 5–8. Pearl decides to make a robot for the school science fair. Wagner has many ideas but never gets around to making anything. Pearl lets Wagner help make a "trash-eating robot." When a judge comes around, their robot falls apart. Wagner slips inside the robot and surprises the judge when she returns. The two friends don't win a prize. Later on, after Wagner insults Pearl's green socks, he cleverly uses the robot to apologize. This is the first book in the Pearl and Wagner series.

Fun Moments: When the judge approaches the robot for the second time, Wagner uses a robot voice to tell the judge, "YOU HAVE A NICE SMILE . . . AND SUCH PRETTY EYES." The judge is flattered, but when she opens the robot, we see the very tip of Wagner's nose peeking out.

Moser, Lisa. *The Monster in the Backpack.*
Illustrated by Noah Z. Jones. Candlewick, 2006.

Ages 5–8. Annie discovers a small monster in her new school backpack. The monster has eaten Annie's school lunch, except for the carrots. "They make me burp." Annie is worried when the monster rips up her homework, but she learns he did it to make confetti for "the Annie-Is-Great Parade."

Fun Moments: When Annie first discovers the monster, he complains that she didn't knock before opening her backpack. When she wonders how she's supposed to do that, he replies, "Next time, ring the doorbell."

Root, Phyllis. *Mouse Goes Out.* **Illustrated by James Croft. Candlewick, 2002.**

Ages 3–5. The four short stories in this very simplest of easy readers features a little mouse. The first story finds Mouse jumping in bigger and bigger puddles. The last puddle shows him no longer jumping but swimming. The last two stories show Mouse camping and playing in the snow.

Fun Moments: Mouse goes fishing in the second story. He catches a boot, a stick, and a fish. He throws them all back. Then he catches a BIG fish. "The big fish throws Mouse back."

Silverman, Erica. *Cowgirl Kate and Cocoa.*
Illustrated by Betsy Lewin. Harcourt, 2005.

Ages 5–8. Cowgirl Kate has several small adventures with her talking horse, Cocoa. In the first story, Cocoa doesn't want to wear horseshoes. We see him trying on cowboy boots instead. When Cowgirl Kate is upset about her rope twirling, she convinces Cocoa to pretend to be a cow. "I'm much too smart to be a cow." She tells him she'll provide pizza if he goes along with it. "'Okay,' he said. 'I'll be a cow. But I will not say moo.'" This is the first book in the Cowgirl Kate and Cocoa series.

Fun Moments: The two friends play hide-and-seek. Cowgirl Kate hides and waits a long time for Cocoa to find her. She finds him in a cornfield, where he informs her that he likes his new game better. "It's called . . . hide-and-*eat*."

Thomas, Shelley Moore. *Good Night, Good Knight.*
Illustrated by Jennifer Plecas. Dutton, 2000.

Ages 5–8. While standing guard at the castle, the Good Knight hears a very loud roar coming from the forest. He jumps on his horse and investigates. "Clippety-clop. Clippety-clop." He finds a dragon, draws his sword, and then notices the dragon is wearing pajamas. The dragon asks for a glass of water and then climbs into bed. The

Good Knight returns to the castle. He hears another roar, and "Clippety-clop. Clippety-clop," he finds another dragon, who asks for a bedtime story. The first dragon asks for another glass of water. This scenario is played out a third time when another dragon requests a bedtime song. This is the first book in the Good Knight series.

Fun Moments: The Good Knight makes one last trip to the cave. The dragons want a goodnight kiss. They line up, eyes closed, lips puckered.

Underwood, Deborah. *Pirate Mom.*
Illustrated by Stephen Gilpin. Random House, 2006.

Ages 5–8. Pete's mother is hypnotized by the Amazing Marco. "When I clap my hands, you will be a pirate." Before he can bring her back, Marco is rushed to the hospital, where his wife is having a baby. Pirate Mom picks a fight with a neighbor, calls another neighbor a bilge rat, and steals "underwear from Mrs. Burt's clothesline."

Fun Moments: Mom dons a scarf, an eye patch, and Pete's pet parrot, and swishes "a wooden spoon at the mailman." "'Arrr!' said Pirate Mom." "'Arrrrrrgh!' said Pete."

Weeks, Sarah. *Baa-Choo!* Illustrated by Jane Manning. HarperCollins, 2004.

Ages 4–7. Sam the lamb tries to sneeze. "Baa . . . ahh . . . No *choo.*" He's upset that "this sneeze will never do" without the "choo." Gwen the hen tries to help by tickling his nose with a feather. Sig the pig sprinkles pepper in front of an electric fan. Franny Nannygoat kicks up dust. Finally, the animals try all three tricks at once. "Sam the lamb let out a sneeze that raised the roof and shook the trees."

Fun Moments: The final illustration shows that Sam blew the other characters up into a tree and onto a roof. They respond with a "Bless you!"

Willems, Mo. *I Am Invited to a Party!* Hyperion, 2007.

Ages 4–7. Piggie is invited to a party and asks her friend Gerald the Elephant to accompany her. Piggie has never been to a party and is not sure how to dress. Gerald says, "I *know* parties." Gerald dons a top hat and grabs a cane. Piggie wears an evening gown. They worry that it might be a pool party. In addition to their fancy clothes, they put on swimsuits, inner tubes, and a snorkel and mask. Later on, they add a cape and cowboy hat for a potential costume party. When they finally arrive at the party, all of the other guests are also wearing fancy clothes, swim gear, and costumes all at once. Piggie says, "You *do* know parties!" This is one of the books in the popular Elephant and Piggie series.

Fun Moments: Every once in a while, Gerald and Piggie joyously dance and shout, "Party! Party! Party! Party!"

In addition to the titles listed above, the following easy-reader series, which began publication pre-2000 and continued into the following decade, are also highly recommended:

- Amelia Bedelia series by Peggy and Herman Parish
- Henry and Mudge series by Cynthia Rylant
- Minnie and Moo series by Denys Cazet
- Mr. Putter and Tabby series by Cynthia Rylant

13

GRAPHIC NOVELS/ MANGA

Bliss, Harry. *Luke on the Loose.* **Toon Books, 2009.**

Ages 5–8. A little boy named Luke is in Central Park with his father when all of a sudden, he takes off after some pigeons. We follow Luke as he and the pigeons startle a dog and its owner, cross the Brooklyn Bridge, zip through a sidewalk café, and disrupt kids at an ice-cream stand. Luke eventually crawls onto the roof of a building and is rescued by the fire department. The last picture shows Luke and his father back in the park. Luke is reaching for some pigeons, but he is now wearing a leash.

Fun Moments: One alley has a wanted poster for the Incredible Hulk. As Luke tears through the café, he interrupts a man proposing to his girlfriend. After the chaos has passed, the man asks, "But Sofi . . . When you say 'EEK! AAAH! HELP! HELP!' is that a YES?"

Davis, Eleanor. *The Secret Science Alliance and the Copycat Crook.* **Bloomsbury, 2009.**

Ages 9–12. Julian Calendar attends a new school. Outwardly, he's a nerd. But inwardly—he's an Ultra Nerd. He is surprised to learn that the school's best athlete and "the most notorious girl" in school are also scientific geniuses. Together, they form the Secret Science Alliance. They use inventions such as the "Pop Open Kick Me Sign," the "Secret Squirt Watch Filled with Stink Ink," and the "Glue Bomb" against the evil Dr. Wilhelm Stringer.

Fun Moments: Julian tries to show his new classmates that he's normal by declaring, "I enjoy popular activities such as 'hanging out' at the local shopping mall and watching sports on TV." His cover is blown when his teacher asks, "What can you tell me about propellers?" Julian sleepily replies, "The propeller spinning creates a pressure difference, which causes air to be accelerated through the blades. This generates thrust and pushes the vehicle forward . . . in accordance with the first law . . ." Julian comes to and notices everyone looking at him.

Davis, Eleanor. *Stinky.* Toon Books, 2008.

Ages 6–9. A small monster named Stinky is proud of his smelly swamp and cave. He is a bit nervous about the nearby town. "Towns have kids . . . and kids don't like swamps. They like to take baths!" One kid named Nick, however, enjoys the swamp and builds a tree house in it. Stinky tries to scare the kid away by placing his overgrown toad, Wartbelly, in the tree house. Nick loves Wartbelly and calls it Daisy. Nick eventually saves Stinky from the Bottomless Pit, and the two become friends.

Fun Moments: The small woodland animals and birds that live near Stinky's cave have clothespins on their noses and beaks.

Elder, Joshua. *Mail Order Ninja, Vol. 1.* Illustrated by Erich Owen. Spotlight, 2009.

Ages 10–12. Timmy wins a contest and receives a real live ninja named Yoshido Jiro. The biographical information about Jiro states that he "once had a promising music career and was dubbed the 'Japanese Barry Manilow' by critics." Timmy's parents inform their son that "owning a ninja is a big responsibility. Remember what happened with the iguana?" Timmy says who knew the iguana "would just explode like that?" The ninja helps Timmy deal with school bullies and win the school election. "Timmy = 984, Felicity = 2, Seymour Butts = 3." This is the first book in the U.S. edition series.

Fun Moments: While Timmy is explaining to his parents that his ninja wouldn't hurt a fly, the ninja is smashing a fly in the background. "Okay, so that was a bad example, but please, Mom . . ."

Gownley, Jimmy. *Amelia Rules: The Whole World's Crazy.* Simon and Schuster, 2003.

Ages 9–11. Amelia's parents are divorced. Amelia and her mother move in with her aunt Tanner. She slowly learns that her new friends—Reggie, Pajamaman, and her "frenemy" Rhonda—are the school nerds. "Now I'm a Nerd by association!" The four of them play superhero games and eventually hook up with other kids who are just as inventive with their imaginations. This is the first book in the Amelia Rules series.

Fun Moments: Reggie matter-of-factly explains that the "sneeze barf" is also known as "Sneezicus Barfona."

Guibert, Emmanuel. *Sardine in Outer Space 4.*
Illustrated by Joann Sfar and Walter Pezzali. First Second, 2007.

Ages 9–11. Sardine has intergalactic adventures with her space-pirate uncle Captain Yellow Shoulder, her cousin Little Louie, and her black cat. They frequently encounter their nasty adversaries Supermuscleman, who is the Chief Executive Dictator of the Universe, and his mad-scientist henchman, Doc Hrok. This is one of many collections in the Sardine in Outer Space series.

Fun Moments: This particular volume is highlighted here because of the fun opening story, titled "Under the Bed." Sardine heads under the bed and finds the leaping sheep "who leap over your bed at night"; the sheep's sheepdog, Shep, who is manning a "Lost and Found" station; and Nightmurray, the monster under the bed, who starts crying. Sardine transfers Nightmurray to Supermuscleman's bed and the leaping sheep over to Doc Hrok's bed.

Harper, Charise Mericle. *Fashion Kitty.* **Hyperion, 2005.**

Ages 8–10. The Kittie family, a family of cats, is unusual. They have a pet mouse named Mousie, aka Phoebe Frederique. The Kittie family members are all vegetarian. One of the daughters, Kiki, is Fashion Kitty. Kiki was hit on the head by a pile of fashion magazines at the same time that she was making a birthday wish and blowing out the candles. In this, her first adventure, Fashion Kitty saves someone from committing a fashion faux pas. This is the first book in the Fashion Kitty series.

Fun Moments: There's a two-page spread on "boys don't give two hoots about fashion." Various boys give their reasons. "I wear the same thing every day. But my mom makes me change my socks and my underwear" and "This is my favorite shirt. I've been wearing it for three years. It's a little short."

Holm, Jennifer L. *Babymouse: Queen of the World.*
Illustrated by Matthew Holm. Random House, 2005.

Ages 7–9. Babymouse is obsessed about attending Felicia Furrypaws's slumber party. Once she does get an invitation and goes to it, she's bored. She then becomes upset when Felicia makes cracks about Babymouse's friend Wilson. This is the first book in the Babymouse series.

Fun Moments: In one of Babymouse's many imagination scenes, she pictures herself as Babymouserella. Her fairy godmother states, "I prefer 'Fairy Godweasel.'"

Kitamura, Satoshi. *Comic Adventures of Boots*. Farrar Straus Giroux, 2002.

Ages 5–8. A cat named Boots stars in three stories in this picture-book-formatted graphic novel. The first story shows Boots tricking the other cats so they have to move off a wall and make space for him. The second story shows a duck saving Boots from drowning. Boots learns to swim afterward and also asks the duck to teach him how to fly. The last story finds Boots and his cat friends playing a game similar to charades.

Fun Moments: In the last story, "Let's Play a Guessing Game," different cats act as a penguin, a cat hanging on to a cliff, a rabbit in its burrow, an owl, and a dog ("'Max at the Maxwells' to be precise"). When one cat makes a goofy face to act as a chameleon, we see him with his face screwed up saying, "Oh, no! I can't put my face back."

Konami, Kanata. *Chi's Sweet Home, Vol. 1*. Vertical, 2010.

Ages 8–10. Chi is a lost little kitten taken in by a young couple with a small boy. She gets her name from being trained to use the kitty box. The family desperately tries to find a home for Chi because their lease forbids pets. Chi has interesting inner dialogue. "Pwease, no more. I'm gonna pway dead." Her thoughts about her new family and situation make this a good exposure to manga for young children. This is the first collection in the Chi's Sweet Home series.

Fun Moments: Before she catches on to its true purpose, Chi refers to her kitty litter box as her "pwaypen."

Krosoczka, Jarrett J. *Lunch Lady and the Cyborg Substitute*. Knopf, 2009.

Ages 8–11. Three students—Hector, Dee, and Terrance—imagine that their lunch lady is a secret agent. It turns out that she is. Lunch Lady is suspicious of the new substitute teacher because he won't eat her famous French-toast sticks. She enters her secret boiler-room lair behind the cafeteria refrigerator and arms herself with a "Spatu-copter," a combination of a spatula and a helicopter. This is the first book in the Lunch Lady series.

Fun Moments: Lunch Lady also has a spork phone, chicken-nugget bombs, and fish-stick nunchaku to help her fight evildoers.

Lechner, John. *Sticky Burr: Adventures in Burrwood Forest*. Candlewick, 2007.

Ages 6–9. Sticky Burr is a unique burr. He'd rather paint and play his ukulele. Scurvy Burr, a bully, tries to get Sticky Burr kicked out of the village. Sticky Burr saves the day by leading a pack of wild dogs away from his friends. The sequel is *Sticky Burr: The Prickly Peril* (Candlewick, 2007).

Fun Moments: Sticky's friend Mossy Burr takes karate lessons from a grasshopper. She tells her instructor, "Thank you, Grasshopper," a reference to the old *Kung Fu* television series.

Morse, Scott. *Magic Pickle*. Graphix/Scholastic, 2008.

Ages 9–12. Jo Jo wakes up when a superpowered pickle bursts through her bedroom floor. The pickle is called Weapon Kosher and was created fifty years earlier by Doctor Formaldehyde. Both Jo Jo and Weapon Kosher battle evil superpowered vegetables known as the Brotherhood of Evil Produce. The climax takes place in the school cafeteria, where Jo Jo starts a food fight. The duo is able to stop the evil Romaine Gladiator by throwing him into a garbage disposal. This is the first book in the Magic Pickle series.

Fun Moments: When Jo Jo first encounters Weapon Kosher, she's wearing "footsie jammies." After their first battle with the Brotherhood of Evil Produce, Weapon Kosher drops Jo Jo off at her school bus stop. She hides from the other kids. "I will not be seen in public in footsie jammies."

Petrucha, Stefan. *Harry Potty and the Deathly Boring*. Illustrated by Rick Parker. Papercutz, 2010.

Ages 10–14. Whiny Stranger, aka Hermione, gives a recap of the first Harry Potter books with her magic spell "Rememberallthisstufficis!" We also see final book played out. Throughout this parody, we find the various Harry Potter characters—Headmaster Always Dumb-As-A-Door, Don Measley, Earwig the owl, Haggard, Frappe (Snapes), the Sorting Sock, and Valuemart, aka "He-Whose-Prices-Can't-Be-Beat."

Fun Moments: During the recap of the first book, we learn that Valuemart has survived by appearing on the "butt of the nervous Defense Against Dark Farts Professor Squirrel." Also, the scar on Harry's forehead keeps changing throughout the book.

Pilkey, Dav. *The Adventures of Ook and Gluk, Kung-Fu Cavemen from the Future*. Scholastic, 2010.

Ages 9–12. The boys from the Captain Underpants series—George and Harold—have created their own comic book, complete with misspellings, of two kids who "lived way back in the year 500,001 B.C. in a village called Caveland, Ohio." They battle the evil Chief Goppernopper, whose ancestor comes from the future through a time portal to plunder ancient Earth of its natural resources.

Fun Moments: The "Cavemonics" lessons at the end of the book teach readers how to talk like cavemen. For example, "My Grandmother doesn't think this book belongs in the school library" turns into "Grandma no fun" in caveman talk.

Pilkey, Dav. *The Adventures of Super Diaper Baby*. Scholastic, 2002.

Ages 9–12. This offering by Pilkey's characters George and Harold gives the origin of Super Diaper Baby. He gained superpowers when he went out a hospital window because the doctor gave him a hearty slap. "Hey, I said I was sorry. Jeez!" The baby fell into a container of superpower juice held by Deputy Dangerous. Later on, when Deputy Dangerous tries to drain Super Diaper Baby of his powers with the transfer helmet and the Danger-Crib 2000, Super Diaper Baby has a messy diaper and—yes, Deputy Dangerous is turned into a piece of poo. This is the first book in the Super Diaper Baby series.

Fun Moments: Super Diaper Baby and Diaper Dog fly to the planet Uranus. A sign reads, "Welcome to Uranus. Please don't make fun of our name."

Proimos, James. *The Many Adventures of Johnny Mutton*. Harcourt, 2001.

Ages 9–11. A baby sheep is left on the doorstep of Momma Mutton, and she decides to raise it as a human child. "Momma's weak eyes and warm heart kept her from even noticing." Johnny stands out by bringing marshmallows to his teacher instead of an apple. For Halloween, he dresses as a runny nose. The other kids make fun of him except for Gloria Crust, who is dressed as a giant box of tissues. At one point, Johnny calls his mother mean because she spends time on her tuba lessons instead of helping him practice for a spelling bee. However, when asked to spell "Love," Johnny responds with "M-O-M-M-A." This is the first book in a series.

Fun Moments: Momma pulls a potato out of Johnny's dirty ear, and he says, "Get out!"

Reynolds, Aaron. *Joey Fly, Private Eye, in Creepy Crawly Crime*. Illustrated by Neil Numberman. Holt, 2009.

Ages 9–11. This crime-noir graphic novel features a sleuth who has been asked to find a butterfly's missing pencil case. With his brand-new assistant, the young scorpion Sammy Stingtail, the fly detective questions a ladybug named Gloria and a mosquito named Flittany. This is the first book in the Joey Fly, Private Eye series.

Fun Moments: Flittany calls Joey Fly a pinhead. Joey's narrative voice-over says, "She had been trying to insult me, but the laugh was on her. My head really is the size of a pin."

Robbins, Trina. *Chicagoland Detective Agency: The Drained Brains Caper*. Illustrated by Tyler Page. Graphic Universe, 2010.

Ages 9–12. Megan Yamamura slowly makes friends with Raf Hernandez at his mother's pet-supply shop, but only after he tells her, "Amscray, go away, and don't let the door hit you on the way out!" She's persistent, though, and when she's captured by the evil Dr. Vorshak, who disguised herself as a school cook in order to control the minds of the students, it's Raf who rescues her. They both free a talking dog named Bradley. This is the first book in the Chicagoland Detective Agency series.

Fun Moments: Bradley learned to talk by watching old detective movies. His first words were "You . . . doidy . . . rats . . ."

Sonishi, Kenji. *Leave It to PET: The Misadventures of a Recycled Super Robot.* Viz Kids, 2009.

Ages 9–12. PET is a tiny super robot transformed from a plastic bottle that was recycled by nine-year-old Noboru. PET promises to help Noboru in any way to show gratitude for being recycled. The trouble is that PET never comes through with his assignments. Noboru captures a grasshopper and wants PET to hold it for him. Unfortunately, PET pops the grasshopper in a container with a praying mantis. After the praying mantis eats the grasshopper, PET develops a "Pet-Bio-Regeneration Project!" He genetically re-creates the grasshopper—and then pops him back in with the praying mantis. The praying mantis eats the grasshopper . . . again.

Fun Moments: PET teaches Noboru the following distress call: "Pa-Pi-Pu-Pe! Pi-Pu-Pe-Po! Po-Pu-Pe-Pa PET! One tiny slip-up and it won't work!" Of course, when Noboru is threatened by bullies, he can't remember the overly complex distress call sequence. "Pa-Po-Pi-Pu? Po-Pu-Pe-Po?"

Spiegelman, Nadja, and Trade Loeffler. *Zig and Wikki in Something Ate My Homework.* Toon Books, 2010.

Ages 6–8. Two aliens land on Earth to complete Zig's homework assignment: get a pet for the class zoo. They try to catch a fly but it gets away. They also encounter dragonflies, a frog, and a raccoon. When the raccoon turns on them, they quickly take off. They are sad that they didn't complete their homework assignment. Then they notice the fly had flown into the spaceship. Mission accomplished.

Fun Moments: Wikki dresses up like a cowboy to catch the frog. The two aliens wind up on a lily pad. Wikki says, "I tied this rope to its leg!" The moment Zig says, "You did WHAT?" the frog, who is underwater, takes off, pulling the lily pad.

Spires, Ashley. *Binky the Space Cat.* Kids Can, 2009.

Ages 6–8. Binky is a house cat who believes he needs to protect his humans from "aliens." The aliens are really bugs. Binky joins F.U.R.S.T., which stands for "Felines of the Universe Ready for Space Travel." Binky trains hard, wearing a bandana and kicking a hanging "pretend alien." He builds a rocket ship but finds it painful to leave his humans. "No more Binky, Space Cat Extraordinaire." After swallowing a fly, he realizes that he made the right choice, because "his humans are utterly helpless without him." The sequel is *Binky to the Rescue* (Kids Can, 2010).

Fun Moments: The copyright page contains the following announcement: "No aliens, bugs, or Space Cats were harmed in the making of this book. Okay, a mosquito was batted away a little too enthusiastically, and a fruit fly drowned under slightly suspicious circumstances, but that's all. Space Cat's honor."

Steinberg, D. J. *The Adventures of Daniel Boom (aka Loud Boy): Game On!* Illustrated by Brian Smith. Grosset and Dunlap, 2009.

Ages 9–11. A group of kids have "pretty extraordinary abilities." They constantly fight "an international web of cranky people known as Kid Rid." The villain known as Old Fogey has a plan to digitally insert kids into a popular computer game called Pig Planet. The final device that the villains need looks like a banana. This is the third book in the Adventures of Daniel Boom (aka Loud Boy) series.

Fun Moments: Uncle Stanley, who is a good guy, has the banana. He asks the kids to meet him at the zoo, where he is disguised as an ape. When the bad guy appears, Uncle Stanley is in the enclosed glass cage dressed up as an ape. He is holding up cue cards for Daniel Boom, who is being interrogated by Old Fogey.

Townsend, Michael. *Kit Feeny: On the Move.* Knopf, 2009.

Ages 8–10. Kit moves from the country to town and leaves behind his best friend, Arnold. He decides to give his classmates an "Arnold test" to see who will be his new best friend. Unfortunately, he runs into Devon the Comedian, a bully. Kit cleverly thinks of a way to deal with Devon and learns that, although no one will replace Arnold, he can still make new friends. This is the first book in the Kit Feeny series.

Fun Moments: Kit makes a comic book with Arnold. It is titled *The Great Gummy Fish Disaster: A True Story* and recounts the time Kit and Arnold poured Jell-O powder into his sisters' goldfish bowl and then set the whole thing in the refrigerator.

Venable, Colleen A. F. *Hamster and Cheese.* Illustrated by Stephanie Yue. Graphic Universe, 2010.

Ages 6–9. Sasspants the guinea pig is mistakenly taken for a private investigator when the *g* in *pig* on the sign outside her cage falls off (thus saying "GUINEA PI"). She lives with several other animals at Mr. Venezi's Pets and Stuff pet store. She is asked to solve the mystery of Mr. Venezi's stolen sandwiches. The hamster who hires

Sasspants is worried that he will be blamed. Mr. Venezi is slightly confused because he thinks the hamsters are koalas. This is the first book in the Guinea PIG, Pet Shop Private Eye series.

Fun Moments: Sasspants interviews the fish as eyewitnesses to the crime. Their responses are all over the place. One states, "I can describe the thief," while another says, "I like bread." Based on their collective comments, the sketch artist comes up with a drawing of the stolen sandwich instead of the thief.

In addition to the titles listed above, Jeff Smith's Bone series, which began in the 1990s, is highly recommended.

14

CHAPTER BOOKS

Anderson, M. T. *Jasper Dash and the Flame-Pits of Delaware*. Simon and Schuster, 2009.

Ages 10–13. Jasper and his two pals, Katie and Lily, head off to the mountains, jungles, dinosaurs, cannibals, and monsters of Delaware—yes, that Delaware. Jasper's evil archnemesis, Bobby Spandrel, has taken over the lost monastery of Vbngoom, a special place for Jasper. The three heroes humorously disagree with each other. When a dinosaur is chasing them, Jasper insists it's a *Tyrannosaurus rex*. Katie remembers from her school report that it's an *Allosaurus*. Jasper: "While I respect your hypothesis—," Katie: "La la la la la! Not listening!" This is the third book in the Pals in Peril series, also known as M. T. Anderson's Thrilling Tales.

Laugh-Out-Loud Selection: Read the first two chapters. Our heroes live in a town so boring that the townsfolk are fanatical about the school's Stare-Eyes team. Opponents stare at each other, and the first one to blink loses.

Ardagh, Philip. *A House Called Awful End*. Holt, 2002.

Ages 10–12. When his parents come down with a horrible disease, Eddie Dickens is forced to live with Mad Uncle Jack and Mad Aunt Maud. On the way to their house, Eddie is mistaken for a runaway orphan and is forced to live at St. Horrid's Home for Grateful Orphans. One reviewer nailed it when she commented that the book is a combination of Charles Dickens, Roald Dahl, and Lemony Snicket. This is the first book in the Eddie Dickens trilogy.

Laugh-Out-Loud Selection: Read episode 10, "Oh, Dear! Oh, Dear! Oh, Dear!" Eddie finds himself in a room with a large rat at the orphanage. The narrator goes on a long, funny tangent about how St. Horrid got his name. When Mrs. Cruel-Streak enters Eddie's room, he makes a daring escape.

Barrows, Annie. *Ivy and Bean and the Ghost That Had to Go.* Chronicle, 2006.

Ages 8–10. Ivy and Bean are good friends. They try to sign a blood oath, but they don't want to attract vampire bats. Instead, they "goosh" gobs of spit and make an "oath of liquids." They both get carried away with rumors of a ghost in the girls' bathroom at their school. They decide to give the ghost little presents, such as a hairclip and a fossil. They flush the "presents" down the toilet. They are caught by a mean teacher, but the toilet overflows at that moment, and the teacher runs for the janitor. "At least there's no you-know-what in it." This is the second book in the Ivy and Bean series.

Laugh-Out-Loud Selection: Read the chapter titled "Sneaky Bean." Ivy and Bean are adding different ingredients to their potion. Bean's sister, Nancy, is yelling at Bean from across the street. "YOU'D BETTER GET OVER HERE RIGHT NOW OR YOU'LL BE SORRY." Bean yells back, "I'M ALREADY SORRY ABOUT HOW STUPID YOU LOOK IN THOSE SHORTS!"

Beaty, Andrea. *Attack of the Fluffy Bunnies.* Amulet, 2010.

Ages 9–11. Joules and Kevin's parents have sent the twins to Camp Whatsitooya on the shores of Lake Whatsosmelly. "Mr. and Mrs. Rockman were on their way to the International SPAMathon in Cheekville, Pennsylvania." The camp owner and counselors are replaced by "fierce, large, ugly, and ferocious furballs known as Fierce, Large, Ugly, and Ferocious. Fluffs for short." The kids must stop the alien rabbits from taking over the planet.

Laugh-Out-Loud Selection: Read chapters 6 and 7. We meet the twins and their parents. Their mother is excited that her children will be at Camp Whatsitooya. "'And they even have a spa,' said Mrs. Rockman. 'See? There's even a picture!' 'It's an outhouse,' said Joules. 'It's rustic!' said her mother. 'What could be better?'" Readers also learn more than they want to know about Spam. At the end of chapter 7, there's a chart. The author tells the reader to read the chart. "We'll amuse ourselves by singing while you read. La la la la la la . . ."

Benton, Jim. *Let's Pretend This Never Happened.*
Scholastic, 2004.

Ages 10–12. Jamie records events in what she calls her "Dumb Diary." She feels threatened by the pretty girl Angeline and is also worried about what kind of nickname Mike Pinsetti will bestow on her. This is the first book in the Dear Dumb Diary series.

Laugh-Out-Loud Selection: Read the first diary entries, through "Sunday 08 (late-breaking news)." The opening entry describes Jamie playing with her pet beagle, Stinker, and doing the thing where you pretend to throw the ball and don't actually throw it. "When I finally realized I hadn't thrown the ball yet, I had probably done it about a hundred and forty times. Stinker was a little cross-eyed and foamy." Later, she refers to Angeline as "Princess Turd of Turdsylvania" and relates how she has to eat her mother's cooking or hear a lecture about the "hungry children in Wheretheheck-istan." The selection ends with Jamie telling Isabella that her lip gloss is actually a roll-on deodorant. "Friends tell friends they're wearing antiperspirants on their mouths."

Benton, Jim. *Lunch Walks among Us.* Simon and Schuster, 2003.

Ages 8–11. Franny K. Stein is a little girl who is a mad scientist, even though the rest of her family is normal. She keeps bats in her attic bedroom as well as "a whole bunch of electrical gizmos that Franny had made all by herself, a tarantula cage, a snake house, and her flying piranhas." She makes an effort to become a normal girl so that she can fit in with her classmates. When a Pumpkin-Crab Monster kidnaps her teacher, Franny resorts to her namesake's talents and creates a Lunch-Meat Creature to save the day. This is the first book in the Franny K. Stein series.

Laugh-Out-Loud Selection: Read chapter 9, "Lunch Doesn't Agree with Me." Something is growing in the classroom trash can. Franny finds out what her classmates have added to the can. She says, "That was close. Well, as long as NOBODY put any unstable industrial waste in there, we should be fine." One boy remembers that he "put some unstable industrial waste in there." The Pumpkin-Crab Monster is created. Continue reading chapter 10, "That's No Jack-O-Lantern." The monster kidnaps Franny's teacher, Miss Shelly (another nod to the Frankenstein legend). A boy wets his pants. The kids are running around. "'We need a fireman,' one girl said. 'We need a superhero,' one boy said. 'We need dry pants,' said you-know-who."

Bolger, Kevin. *Sir Fartsalot Hunts the Booger.* Razorbill, 2008.

Ages 9–12. A very old knight named Sir Fartsalot arrives at the castle in the Kingdom of Armpit. Young Prince Harry mischievously tells the knight about the terrifying Booger. Not realizing that he is the victim of a joke, Sir Fartsalot sets up to do battle.

"'Where might one find one of these Boogers?' 'Oh, you never know,' Harry said. 'Sometimes they can be right under your nose. So to speak.'" The prank backfires on Harry when his father, King Reginald the Not Very Realistic, sends his naughty son to accompany Sir Fartsalot. Along the way, they have many battles with ogres, rocs, giants—even a castle full of princesses. Harry grows to admire the courageous knight and regrets his poor behavior. Despite the frequent potty-style jokes, Bolger includes many witty puns and other examples of wordplay throughout the adventure.

Laugh-Out-Loud Selection: Read the first two chapters, which describe the setting and introduce many key characters. The palace is buzzing with stories about Sir Fartsalot. "I heard he once beat 12 trolls single-handedly in a fight." "I heard that, too. Only it was a *dozen* trolls."

Clements, Andrew. *Jake Drake, Class Clown*. Simon and Schuster, 2002.

Ages 9–11. Jake sees school as his full-time job and his teacher as his boss. He tweaks his role, however, when his class gets a student teacher, Miss Bruce. She is a no-nonsense teacher, and the class is afraid of her. Jake decides to become the class clown, and he works hard to get a smile out of Miss Bruce. Unfortunately, his superloud burp and follow-up comment—"Pardon me. It must have been that frog I ate for breakfast!"—disrupt the entire class and send Miss Bruce running out of the room in tears. This is the first book in the Jake Drake series.

Laugh-Out-Loud Selection: Read chapter 3, "Scared Silly." Jake is upset that Miss Bruce is overly harsh during the class spelling bee. He stands up to spell "mouse" and decides to use a high squeaky voice for his reply. "Mouse: m-i-c-k-e-y; mouse." Move on to chapter 6, "Mr. Funny Bone." Jake is trying a knock-knock joke on his younger sister, who doesn't understand the concept of knock-knocks.

Cowell, Cressida. *How to Train Your Dragon*. Little, Brown, 2004.

Ages 9–12. Hiccup Horrendous Haddock III is the heir to the Viking clan, but he's puny, and the other boys, including Dogsbreath and Snotlout, disrespect him. To pass their initiation, each of the boys must capture a dragon. Hiccup grabs Toothless, the smallest of all dragons. Hiccup discovers he has one talent none of the other boys has—he can talk "dragonese." When the clan is in danger from two sea dragons, Hiccup saves the day. This is the first book in the How to Train Your Dragon series.

Laugh-Out-Loud Selection: Read the short insert, "How to Train Your Dragon," by Professor Yobbish. This book within the book is published by Big Axe Books. We find out that it is a library copy, and the date-due slip has a warning from the "Hairy Scary Librarian." The brief author biography tells us Yobbish has also written books on killer whales and sharks and is currently writing a book about butterflies. The back cover has review quotes: "'This book changed my life.' Squidface the Terrible." We also learn the price of the book: "1 smallish chicken, 20 oysters."

Curtis, Christopher Paul. *Mr. Chickee's Funny Money.* Wendy Lamb, 2005.

Ages 10–12. Steven is given a quadrillion dollar bill by his blind, elderly neighbor Mr. Chickee. The bill has a picture of soul singer James Brown on it. Steven learns that this bill is real and there are only five in circulation. Treasury Agent Foondoo tries everything he can to retrieve the quadrillion dollar bill. The sequel is *Mr. Chickee's Messy Mission* (Random House, 2007).

Laugh-Out-Loud Selection: Read chapter 3. Steven asks his father how much is a one followed by fifteen zeroes. His father tells him to look it up in the dictionary. The dictionary seemingly talks to Steven. When Steven checks out the copyright page, he reads, "You're not a librarian; what are you doing on this page?" Later on, the dictionary calls him "diminutive" and a "dunce" and closes with "Don't take it personally, but I call 'em like I see 'em!"

DiCamillo, Kate. *Mercy Watson to the Rescue.* Candlewick, 2005.

Ages 6–9. Mr. and Mrs. Watson own a pet pig named Mercy. Mercy loves buttered toast. Mrs. Watson loves making buttered toast for Mercy. They are both having buttered-toast dreams (while Mr. Watson is having a dream about driving a fast car) when they are all awakened by a "Boom" and a "Crack!" The bed is in danger of falling through the second floor. Mercy hops off the bed and heads outside in search of food. The Watsons believe she is going out for help. Mercy shows up next door and startles the elderly Lincoln sisters. While Eugenia is chasing Mercy, the fire department shows up. They hear the Watsons' cries and save the day. Mercy, of course, gets all the credit. This is the first book in the Mercy Watson series.

Laugh-Out-Loud Selection: Read the entire book; it will only take a few minutes. The funniest lines are when the Watsons insist that Eugenia call Mercy "a porcine wonder."

Fleming, Candace. *The Fabled Fourth Graders of Aesop Elementary School.* Schwartz and Wade, 2007.

Ages 9–11. This year's fourth-grade class at Aesop Elementary is the naughtiest bunch of students ever. When Mr. Jupiter shows up to be their teacher, he quickly wins them over with his easygoing behavior and worldwide experience. He even accepts their answers to such questions as, "Who can give me the definition of *goblet*?" A student answers, "A small turkey." The sequel is *The Fabled Fifth Graders of Aesop Elementary* (Schwartz and Wade, 2010).

Laugh-Out-Loud Selection: Read the chapter, "Calvin Goes to Kindergarten." Fourth-grader Calvin wishes school was as easy this year as it was for him in kindergarten, "where school was fun and easy." He is sent to the kindergarten room to be a student helper. The kindergarteners give him a hard time because he doesn't know their little rules, such as sitting with pretzel legs. Whenever he complains, "But I'm a fourth grader," no one pays attention. Calvin especially dislikes swishing his bottom to a "gray squirrel" rhyme activity. When he finally returns to the fourth grade, he's dismayed to find his classmates doing the "gray squirrel" rhyme, too.

Griffiths, Andy. *The Day My Butt Went Psycho.* Scholastic, 2003.

Ages 10–12. Griffiths's introductory warning states, "If you are a parent or a teacher or even if you're just over eighteen, put this book down now! You won't like it." Young Zack's butt leaves Zack and leads a revolution of butts against humans. If the title doesn't give an indication of what the entire book is about, sample chapter titles, such as "Stenchgator" and "Methane Madness," will. This is the first book in a trilogy.

Laugh-Out-Loud Selection: Read chapter 2, "The Butt Hunter's Daughter." Zack is attacked by a squadron of flying butts. He's worried they'll gas him. He grabs a tennis racket and starts "thwacking" them. "The butt went hurtling off his racket and into the back of a parked car. BOOM! The explosion was deafening and the force of it knocked Zack over onto his back." When two flying butts attack him from different directions, Zack ducks in time and "the butts [collide] with a thunderous sonic boom." Zack is next attacked by "a cluster butt."

Hale, Bruce. *The Chameleon Wore Chartreuse: From the Tattered Casebook of Chet Gecko, Private Eye.* Harcourt, 2000.

Ages 9–11. Chet Gecko is a private eye. "I go to fourth grade at Emerson Hicky Elementary. I'm a lizard." On the first day of school, Chet is asked to solve a mystery. Shirley Chameleon's little brother, Billy, is missing. "Shirley stood up. One tearful eye looked at me while her other eye watched a gnat flying above us. Chameleons do that." This is the first book in the Chet Gecko Mystery series.

Laugh-Out-Loud Selection: Read the short chapter 5, "The Messes of Hippopotamia." Chet's first clue is an excuse that Billy's mom supposedly wrote. "Pls xcuze Blly frm skool today. He iz sikk." Chet is anxious to get information from the principal's office, so he raises his hand. "Mr. Ratnose, can I go to the principal's office?" Mr. Ratnose says no. Chet does this two more times before Mr. Ratnose is fed up.

"Absolutely not! You've interrupted me for the last time! Take this note and go straight to the principal's office."

Horvath, Polly. *The Pepins and Their Problems.* **Farrar Straus Giroux, 2004.**

Ages 9–12. The Pepin family and their neighbors have a series of seemingly insurmountable problems. At times throughout the book, the author solicits solutions from the readers. Although some of the situations seem plausible and easily solved by normal folks, there are several problems that defy belief. One day, the Pepins' talking cow gives lemonade instead of milk. This is a problem because the Pepins want to serve cheese cubes to their neighbor Mr. Bradshaw. They decide to put a pear on the plate with the lemonade squares to "trick the eyes." Unfortunately, there isn't a pear to be found.

Laugh-Out-Loud Selection: Read the first chapter, "Toads in Their Shoes." We meet the Pepin family and learn the author's technique of asking the readers for assistance. In this case, the Pepins are wondering why their shoes are filled with toads. Continue reading the next chapter, "Grilled Lemonade Sandwiches, Anyone?" The Pepins find themselves on their roof. Their ladder has fallen down. Their neighbors are kicking aside the ladder and trying to come up with solutions to get the Pepins safely down.

Kinney, Jeff. *Diary of a Wimpy Kid: Greg Heffley's Journal.* **Amulet, 2007.**

Ages 9–13. Greg Heffley keeps a journal of his experience in sixth grade. The drawings Greg adds to the journal are as much fun as his insights. He says he didn't learn anything from last year when sitting by "hot girls," and this is followed by a girl asking him to pass a note (readers see that the note says, "Greg is a dork"). Not only is this the first book in the Diary of a Wimpy Kid series, but it also spawned several imitation series that follow the same format.

Laugh-Out-Loud Selection: Read the last series of entries in the month of November, where Greg's mother tells Greg to try out for the school musical, *The Wizard of Oz*. Greg is happy to get the part of a tree because "1) they don't have to sing and 2) they get to bean Dorothy with apples." Greg dislikes Patty Farrell, the girl who plays Dorothy. Continue reading into the December entries, which cover the play presentation. Greg and the other trees forget their lines, notice an angry Patty Farrell, and start pelting her with apples.

Klise, Kate. *Dying to Meet You.* **Harcourt, 2009.**

Ages 9–12. A cranky famous children's book author, Ignatius B. Grumply, rents an old Victorian mansion to write his first book in twenty years. He is not a fan of his audience. "I happen to write books for children. That doesn't mean I want to see or hear the little monsters when I'm trying to work." Instead of a nice, quiet house, he gets a home already occupied by an eleven-year-old boy and a cat. Ignatius failed to notice that this arrangement was stipulated in the contract. The ghost of an unpublished author also lives in the house. This is the first in the 43 Old Cemetery Road series.

Laugh-Out-Loud Selection: Simply read the introductory cast of characters, which includes Anita Sale, the real-estate agent; E. Gadds, a lawyer; Paige Turner, a publisher; Les and Diane Hope, two paranormal experts; Seymour Hope, their son; Frank N. Beans, a private investigator; and Olive C. Spence, a ghost. You can also mention that the editor of the newspaper in Ghastly, Illinois (the setting), is named Cliff Hanger.

Korman, Gordon. *No More Dead Dogs.* Hyperion, 2000.

Ages 11–14. Eighth-grader Wallace Wallace is the school's football hero. Normally a benchwarmer, he luckily fell on a ball that won the county championship. He is also proud of the fact that he always tells the truth. His book report describes *Old Shep, My Pal* as "the most boring book I've ever read in my entire life." He also complains that the dog always dies. "Go to the library and pick out a book with an award sticker and a dog on the cover. Trust me, that dog is going down." Unfortunately, *Old Shep, My Pal* is his teacher's favorite book. Mr. Fogelman makes Wallace Wallace serve detention by missing football practice and attending rehearsals of the school play— you guessed it—*Old Shep, My Pal.*

Laugh-Out-Loud Selection: Read a section from the second chapter, titled "Enter . . . Rachel Turner." Start with the sentence, "Wallace pulled a few sheets of paper from his backpack and handed them to the director." He has a list of "Eleven Reasons Why *Old Shep, My Pal* is a Terrible Book." He points out the unbelievable dialogue. "I know for a fact that I've never said anything as stupid as, 'Great heavens, this dog has suffered an injury!'" The other cast members want to change the line to "Check it out." Finish the passage with the sentence, "'That's enough rewriting for the day,' Mr. Fogelman decided."

Krieg, Jim. *Griff Carver, Hallway Patrol.* Razorbill, 2010.

Ages 10–13. Imagine famous crime fighters from the 1940s, such as Sam Spade or Philip Marlow, in the body of a seventh-grade member of the Rampart Middle School Patrol Squad. Young Griff Carver takes his job seriously. With the help of his partner, Tommy Rodriguez, the ultimate scout who has earned merit badges in just about everything, the two uncover a fake hall-pass operation.

Laugh-Out-Loud Selection: Read chapter 3. Carver patrols the halls of his new school for the first time and manages to catch the school principal littering. When called a hero, Carver states, "A hero's just a sandwich the cafeteria served us every Wednesday. . . . It was mostly bologna." Carver is also suspicious about the school's most popular student, Marcus Volger. When told every kid in school likes Volger, Carver replies, "Every dog in the world likes to drink antifreeze, too . . . Too bad it's poison."

Lieb, Josh. *I Am a Genius of Unspeakable Evil and I Want to Be Your Class President.* Penguin, 2009.

Ages 11–14. Twelve-year-old Oliver Watson is secretly one of the world's richest masterminds; he just happens to attend seventh grade and live with his parents. His classmates look down on him and don't realize he has unseen bodyguards who punish any would-be bullies. He has the technology to type messages on his English teacher's cigarettes just to mess with his head. But what Oliver wants most of all is the respect of his father. He decides the way to do this is to win the election for class president.

Laugh-Out-Loud Selection: Inform your audience that a child, who is really an evil genius, is trying to make his class president opponents drop out of the race. Read chapter 14, "Oliver Watson's Theater of the Mind Presents Three Plays for Your Amusement." A popular boy drops out of the race when presented with pictures of him eating his boogers. However, a girl named Liz is not intimidated by a thug known as the Motivator. In fact, she thinks the blackmail photos of her dancing in her pajamas and singing into a hairbrush are wonderful. "Can I get more?"

Lowry, Lois. *Gooney Bird Greene.* Houghton Mifflin, 2002.

Ages 8–10. Gooney Bird Greene is the new second-grade student in Mrs. Pidgeon's class. Gooney Bird "likes to be right smack dab in the middle of everything." She regales her teacher and classmates with what seem like larger-than-life stories, but, as Gooney Bird says, "I tell only absolutely true stories." Each story indeed turns out to be true, although not in the way most of her classmates (and we, the readers) expected. Gooney shows great patience and maturity when she is constantly, and humorously, interrupted by the students. This is the first book in the Gooney Bird Greene series.

Laugh-Out-Loud Selection: Read chapter 5. Gooney Bird is late, and her excuse is that she had to direct an orchestra. "Mrs. Pidgeon smiled. 'I hear all sorts of interesting excuses for tardiness, but I have never heard that one before.'" It turns out that a bus carrying members of a concert symphony band was lost and looking for the concert hall. Gooney Bird directed them to the hall, thus, "directing the orchestra."

Lowry, Lois. *The Willoughbys.*
Houghton Mifflin, 2008.

Ages 10–12. The Willoughby children—Timothy; the twins, A and B; and Jane—decide to become orphans and plot to send their parents on a sea voyage. In the meantime, their parents devise a plan for getting rid of the children. The children gain a new nanny, who joins them in an effort to deter potential buyers of their home. They also gain a new baby (found on their doorstep) whom they, in turn, deliver to a wealthy neighbor who is depressed because he lost his wife and son years ago.

Laugh-Out-Loud Selection: Read most of chapter 13, "The Obsequious Postmaster," beginning with the line, "The tiny bell at the top of the door rang as a woman entered with her little boy." The woman is convinced her son knows German. In truth, the boy simply uses "English words and added extra syllables with a vaguely Germanic sound. 'Helloschlimhofen,' the little boy said cheerfully. 'Neisch day, isn't itzenschlitz?'"

Maguire, Gregory. *Leaping Beauty and Other Animal*
Fairy Tales. **HarperCollins, 2004.**

Ages 9–12. Leaping Beauty is a frog version of "Sleeping Beauty." This fractured fairy tale collection also features the following stories: "Goldifox and the Three Chickens," "Hamster and Gerbil," "So What and the Seven Giraffes," "Little Red Robin Hood," "The Three Little Penguins and the Big Bad Walrus," "Cinder-Elephant," and "Rumplesnakeskin."

Laugh-Out-Loud Selection: Read "Cinder-Elephant." When Cinder-Elephant mentions that she wants to go to the prince's ball, her stepmother replies, "The only ball you'll ever go to is the one you'll balance on when I sell you to the circus." Eventually, she goes to the ball wearing two glass pie plates as slippers. After she runs away from the prince, he goes all over the kingdom to "find the one whose foot fit into a glass pie plate." Afterward, we learn Cinder-Elephant's nearly blind father accidentally drives a bus over his former wife's and her daughters' feet. "At last their feet really *did* fit in the glass pie plates."

McDonald, Megan. *Judy Moody.* **Candlewick, 2000.**

Ages 8–10. Judy is in a foul mood her first day of third grade. When her teacher asks her if she's in a bad mood, Judy replies, "ROAR!" Her mood improves when she and her classmates create "Me" collages. The project includes describing your favorite pet and the funniest thing that ever happened to it. Judy buys a Venus flytrap and counts that as her pet. She tricks her brother, Stink, by placing a fake human hand in the toilet. This is the first book in the Judy Moody series. Stink stars in his own series, too.

Laugh-Out-Loud Selection: Read the chapter titled "The T.P. Club." Judy and her friends catch a toad. While she's holding it, she feels something warm and wet. "That toad peed on me!" When the same thing happens to Judy's friend Rocky, they start a new club—the Toad Pee Club. Stink learns about their secret club. Judy and Rocky make Stink hold the toad. Nothing happens. "Oh well. Put the toad back. You can't be in the club." Stink suddenly feels something warm and wet on his hand. He's allowed in the club.

McMullan, Kate. *School! Adventures at the Harvey N. Trouble Elementary School*. Feiwel and Friends, 2010.

Ages 9–11. Fans of Abbott and Costello's routine "Who's on First?" may enjoy the pun-filled adventures that take place during one week at Harvey N. Trouble Elementary School. The characters include a school bus driver named Mr. Stuckinaditch, who consistently gets the bus stuck in a ditch, and Mr. Hugh da Mann, the kindergarten teacher.

Laugh-Out-Loud Selection: Read the opening chapter. Ron Faster gets to school to find his regular teacher, Mrs. Petzgalore, absent. The substitute, Mr. Norman Don't Know, doesn't know where she is (or much else). The class roll call features, among others, Anita Dawg, Izzy Normal, Viola Fuss, and Gladys Friday. It happens to be Abby Birthday's birthday. There's a mess, and the two janitors—Janitor Iquit and Assistant Janitor Quitoo—quit. This all happens during a "hotsy-totsy Monday."

Nolan, Lucy. *Down Girl and Sit: Smarter Than Squirrels*. Marshall Cavendish, 2004.

Ages 7–9. Narrator Down Girl is a dog who lives with her master, Rruff, and next door to her friend Sit. Down Girl wakes up Rruff because she wants to be the first thing he sees in the morning. "Rruff is lucky I woke him when I did. In another hour the alarm clock would have gone off and scared him." Down Girl also successfully chases away the newspaper boy because newspapers are for spanking. "Once again I saved my master from getting spanked." This is the first book in the Down Girl and Sit series.

Laugh-Out-Loud Selection: Read the first two chapters. Down Girl introduces us to her world. We meet her new neighbor Here Kitty Kitty. Down Girl eats everything in sight, including acorns, flowers, sticks, bird seed, a whole sack of dog food, and a pie stolen from the table. She runs behind the couch. "Here's something odd. The couch had somehow gotten smaller."

Palatini, Margie. *Geek Chic: The Zoey Zone*. HarperCollins, 2008.

Ages 9–11. Ten-year-old Zoey is worried that she's not cool. She wishes for a fairy godmother to help her out. One day, she wears her "great-grandpop's fedora" to school. She wears it with a turquoise bowling shirt with the name "Ray" on it as well as "Grabowski's Tool and Die Company." It just so happens that people from the magazine *U GrL* are at the school taking photographs. They get such a big reaction from their readers about Zoey's outfit and her locker contents that the magazine invites the suddenly cool protagonist to write her own column.

Laugh-Out-Loud Selection: Read chapter 2. Zoey and her friend Venus are the last ones in the cafeteria line. Their remaining options are meatloaf and slumgullion. Venus chooses the latter. "She really lives on the edge." There are no seats open except with the Bashleys, the popular girls Ashley and Brittany and their friends, or with Alex Shemtob, who "mostly exhales what he inhales." It's a good idea to wear art smocks when sitting across from him. The girls sit with the Bashleys but are quickly sent away after becoming overly excited about frogs. "Sudden reality check for V and Z. Catching bullfrogs is probably not in any way totally or even semitotally cool or awesome to Ashley and slash or Brittany." They slink to the table with Alex. "It isn't pretty. They are not wearing art smocks."

Paulsen, Gary. *How Angel Peterson Got His Name, and Other Outrageous Tales about Extreme Sports*. Wendy Lamb, 2003.

Ages 11–14. It is author Gary Paulsen's contention that his generation—as youngsters—participated in all sorts of extreme sports long before they became a national craze.

Laugh-Out-Loud Selection: Read a portion of chapter 5, "And Finally, Skateboards, Bungee Jumping, and Other Failures," beginning with the sentence, "To understand what might have been the first bungee jump you have to understand my cousin Harris." Paulsen tells about the time Harris, whom we met in *Harris and Me* (Harcourt, 1993), jumped out the hayloft door in a homemade bungee-jumping-like contraption and snapped back up in the air, straight into a wasps' nest. "'Cut the rope! Cut the rope!' he screamed, but I had no knife and had to untie the end he had tied to the barn and my ability to untie the rope was greatly handicapped by the fact that I was laughing hysterically." Finish the passage where Harris states, "I wouldn't do that again even *without* the wasps."

Peck, Richard. *The Teacher's Funeral: A Comedy in Three Parts*. Dial, 2004.

Ages 11–14. The mean old one-room-schoolhouse teacher Myrt Arbuckle dies in August, and fifteen-year-old Russell is excited. "It was surely too late to find another teacher who'd teach in a place like that." The funeral scene is hilarious. Before the ceremony, Russell is dismayed to learn he has to "wear shoes and clean underdrawers to the funeral. Shoes on a weekday. Underdrawers in August. We fumed." He's also stymied that his seventeen-year-old sister, Tansy, is planning on taking a bath for the funeral. "A bath? . . . It's *Thursday*." Russell is stunned when his sister is named the new teacher.

Laugh-Out-Loud Selection: Read a section of chapter 3, "Me and Lloyd and Charlie Parr," beginning with the line, "I waited for just the right moment: this one." At night, near the creek, Russell tells how grave robbers want the body of Old Man Lichtenberger. He drank so much, he's already "preserved in alcohol." Shortly afterward, Russell's friend Charlie arrives out of the darkness. He pretends to be Old Man Lichtenberger and scares Russell's brother Lloyd. Payback comes later on that evening when Tansy shows up pretending to be the ghost of Myrt Arbuckle, scaring Russell enough to step on hot coals in his attempt to escape.

Peck, Richard. *A Year Down Yonder*. Dial, 2000.

Ages 11–14. Mary Alice spends the year of 1937 with her larger-than-life grandmother. Grandma Dowdel makes the occasional remark about how much tougher life was when she was young. "When I was a girl, we had to walk in our sleep to keep from freezing to death." Grandma also talks about how healthy their little Illinois town is compared to New York. "It's the healthiest spot in Illinois. We had to hang a man to start a graveyard." All of the townsfolk respect Grandma Dowdel, who covers up a kind heart with her gruff exterior. The companion books featuring Grandma Dowdel are *A Long Way from Chicago* (Dial, 1998) and *A Season of Gifts* (Dial, 2009).

Laugh-Out-Loud Selection: Read a section of the chapter titled "Rich Chicago Girl," beginning with the sentence, "The day went straight downhill from there." On her first day at her new school, Mary Alice is terrorized by Mildred Burdick. "Ya owe me a dollar, rich Chicago girl." The two travel to Grandma Dowdel's place to collect the dollar, and when Grandma manages to outfox Mildred out of a horse, Mildred has to walk several miles home without her boots. End the passage with the line, "We sat there at the kitchen table, Grandma and I, while the shadow crept across the linoleum."

Peirce, Lincoln. *Big Nate: In a Class by Himself*. HarperCollins, 2010.

Ages 9–12. Nate is not exactly the most successful student. However, he has big expectations for himself when he receives a fortune cookie that contains the following fortune: "Today you will surpass all others." As he and his friends try to figure out what he will excel at, Nate starts racking up one detention slip after another. When he finally reports to after-school detention, Mrs. Czerwicki informs him, "You appear to have established a new record. . . . Nobody has ever received seven detention slips in one day. Until now." Nate breaks out in a little "Woo! Woo!" dance. This is the first book in the Big Nate series.

Laugh-Out-Loud Selection: Read chapter 5. Nate is almost caught eating his fortune cookie in class; then he makes comments about the morning announcements, runs through his daily school schedule, and shares the nicknames he created for his teachers. "One of my all-time best nicknames for Mrs. Godfrey is Venus de Silo . . . Venus is also the name of a planet. Mrs. Godfrey is a lot like a planet. She's huge and gassy."

Pennypacker, Sara. *The Talented Clementine.* Hyperion, 2007.

Ages 8–10. Clementine is worried when all of the third-graders are assigned to perform in a fund-raising talent show called "The Talent-Palooza Night of the Stars!" She doesn't have a talent to share. She takes quick tap-dancing lessons from a girl named Margaret. When Margaret's tap shoes don't fit, Clementine takes the caps of twenty-four bottles of beer off with pliers and superglues them to the bottom of her sneakers. This is the second book in the Clementine series.

Laugh-Out-Loud Selection: Read the first half of chapter 4. The kids in Clementine's class describe their talents. Maria's act is "Cartwheel Extravaganza," and she demonstrates by crashing into the chalkboard. Another kid's act is called "Cartwheel Wham-o-Rama." He crashes into the hamster cage. Finish the passage with the following lines: "'Now,' my teacher was saying, 'does anyone have an act that *isn't* cartwheeling?' Half the kids put their hands down."

Pratchett, Terry. *The Amazing Maurice and His Educated Rodents.* HarperCollins, 2001.

Ages 11–14. A cat named Maurice and several rats gained the ability to talk after the rats ate some refuse from a Wizard's University dump and Maurice ate one of the rats. They join up with a pipe-playing boy named Keith in this retelling of "The Pied Piper." Trouble erupts when they enter the town of Bad Blintz and try to run their rat-catching scheme.

Laugh-Out-Loud Selection: Read the first chapter. Keith is traveling on a mail coach when they are stopped by a highwayman. "Are there any *wizards* in there?" the robber asks. He goes on to inquire about witches, "heavily armed trolls employed by the mail coach company," werewolves, and vampires. Assured that there aren't, the highwayman pokes his crossbow arrow through the window and says, "Your money *and* your life. It's a two-for-one deal, see?" He hears a noise and freezes. He is covered by rats. And he's mystified to find himself talking to a cat, who says, "Ah, there you are. . . . Went straight up your trouser legs, did they?" The cat, the boy, and the rats wind up robbing the robber. As they leave him behind, the highwayman grabs a sword and runs forward. "Slightly forward, in any case. He wouldn't have hit the ground so hard if someone hadn't tied his bootlaces together."

Pratchett, Terry. *The Wee Free Men: A Story of Discworld.*
HarperCollins, 2003.

Ages 11–14. Tiffany is a young witch who chases the Elf Queen for kidnapping Tiffany's little brother. Helping Tiffany are the Wee Free Men, six-inch "pictsies," with funny, heavy Scottish brogues. In one hilarious scene, the pictsie named No'-as-big-as-Medium-Sized-Jock-but-bigger-than-Wee-Jock-Jock is trying to tell Tiffany the correct way to say his name as well as the fact that the pictsies will be protecting her. This is the first book in the Tiffany Aching series.

   Laugh-Out-Loud Selection: Read a section of chapter 3, "Hunt the Hag," beginning with the sentence, "There was only one place where it was possible for someone in a large family to be private, and that was in the privy." Tiffany is complaining about some fairy-tale characters, such as the "girl who can't tell the difference between a wolf and her grandmother." She notices a sheep being stolen and then catches two strange little men underneath a chicken stealing the eggs. The little men try to explain they thought the eggs were stones and were removing these uncomfortable things from the "puir fowl." Tiffany manages to scare the little men. End the passage with the lines, "That wasn't a lie. In fact, it was completely true."

Rex, Adam. *The True Meaning of Smekday.*
Hyperion, 2007.

Ages 10–14. The Boov alien race has taken over Earth. They celebrate the date of their invasion by calling it Smekday. Eleven-year-old Gratuity (her friends call her "Tip") has lost her mother. She grabs her cat at the last minute (a small detail that has big implications at the end) and drives to Arizona (via Florida), where the humans have been resettled. Along the way, she meets a Boov named J. Lo, who has made a terrible mistake by drawing the attention of another alien race much fiercer than the Boovs.

   Laugh-Out-Loud Selection: Start at the beginning of the section titled "The True Meaning of Smekday, Part 2; or, How I Learned to Stop Worrying and Love the Boov." Gratuity tells how her mother was abducted by the aliens. Gratuity describes her mother to the reader. "When people ask me about her, I say she's very pretty. When they ask if she's smart like me, I say she's very pretty." Gratuity also comments that the greeting-card companies need to make a "Sorry all your friends deserted you after your alien abduction" card.

Riddell, Chris. *Ottoline and the Yellow Cat.* **HarperCollins, 2008.**

Ages 8–10. While her parents are on one of their constant trips, Ottoline lives in a lavish apartment with Mr. Munroe, who resembles Cousin It from *The Addams Family* television show. The two unravel a lost-dog/jewelry-heist operation led by a cat and a cockatoo. The sequel is *Ottoline Goes to School* (HarperCollins, 2009).

Laugh-Out-Loud Selection: Read the first two chapters, including all of the little notes and newspaper accounts. Ottoline lives on the twenty-fourth floor of the Pepperpot Building. She has an "Odd Show" collection. Mr. Munroe shows Ottoline the posters he has found around town. Lapdogs, with names like Wilson Happy-Ears McMurtagh and Fifi Fiesta Funny-Face III, are missing. Ottoline notices clues in the newspaper. Next to several articles about stolen jewelry (the victims all have funny quotes about not being able to talk about the matter) is an advertisement for a lapdog agency. Ottoline and Mr. Munroe disguise themselves and find something suspicious. And no, it's not the sock-stealing bear hiding out in the laundry room.

Scieszka, Jon, ed. *Guys Write for Guys Read.* **Viking, 2005.**

Ages 10–14. Several male children's and young adult authors contributed two- and three-page stories, poems, comic strips, and commentaries about being a boy. Neil Gaiman learned that books are dangerous, Andy Griffiths brags that his dad is better than yours, and one fact about Anthony Horowitz is that he "had a dog called Lucky but accidentally ran it over, so he changed the dog's name to Unlucky."

Laugh-Out-Loud Selection: Read Scieszka's contribution titled "Brothers." He is from a family of five boys. On one trip, they stop at a Stuckey's restaurant and buy a pecan log roll. Their cat eats it once they are back on the road and makes that "awful ack ack ack sound of a cat getting ready to barf." The cat does indeed barf, creating a chain reaction of puking boys, who "spilled out of the puke wagon and fell in the grass, gagging and yelling and laughing until we couldn't laugh anymore." Scieszka repeats this story (listed as "Car Trip") in his autobiography, *Knucklehead: Tall Tales and Mostly True Stories about Growing Up Scieszka* (Viking, 2008).

Seegert, Scott. *How to Grow Up and Rule the World.* **Egmont, 2010.**

Ages 10–14. Vordak the Incomprehensible shares his instruction manual designed to teach readers how to become supervillains. Advice is given on perfecting the perfect evil laugh ("MUAHAHAHAHA!"); creating a supervillain costume ("Black is the color of hopelessness, of oppression. . . . It is also quite slimming"); and constructing evil lairs ("If you live in a state with bottle and can deposits, you receive 5 cents for every one you return. Do the math—20 million cans = *1 million dollars!* MUAHA-HAHAHA!!!").

Laugh-Out-Loud Selection: Read the section in chapter 5 titled "What's in a Name?" Be sure to share the "Supervillain Power Chart." This contains the names of villains, their assumed powers, and what Vordak the Incomprehensible learned was the *actual* reason for their names. For example, it was assumed that Professor Octopus was "equipped with multiple powerful mechanical arms." Actually, we learn he "squirts ink from bellybutton when frightened."

Spratt, R. A. *The Adventures of Nanny Piggins.* Little, Brown, 2010.

Ages 9–12. Nanny Piggins is a chocolate-loving pig whose only job experience is as a flying pig in the circus. She was shot out of a cannon. She is hired by Mr. Green to watch his three children—Derrick, Samantha, and Michael—mostly because he is a cheap man and Nanny Piggins only charges ten cents an hour. The children, of course, love her, and they all work hard to make sure she is not replaced by a regular human nanny.

Laugh-Out-Loud Selection: Read chapter 7, "Nanny Piggins and the Intruder." Nanny Piggins and the children have been playing the game of Murder in the Dark all night long. The reason the game has gone on so long is that they "had simply forgotten to elect a murderer before they started." Nanny Piggins catches a young burglar who has been watching the house for some time, hoping to steal cash or jewelry. Instead of turning the juvenile delinquent over to the authorities, Nanny Piggins comes up with many inventive forms of punishment, including baking "a double-chocolate-chip chocolate mud cake with chocolate icing and chocolate sauce in the middle." Nanny Piggins also makes the thief sand and paint the bathroom. "It [was] a pain persuading Mr. Green to go to work every morning without going to the toilet." He also has to cut down a tree, catch cockroaches, learn to dance the tango, and conjugate verbs. He eventually learns his lesson.

Stadler, Alexander. *Julian Rodriguez: Episode One, Trash Crisis on Earth.* Scholastic, 2008.

Ages 8–10. Julian Rodriguez frequently corresponds with the Mothership. He complains about his Parental Units. They disrupted his sleep state and fed him "intergalactic space sludge," aka oatmeal. He finds it challenging to hide his intellectual superiority from "the mini-brains" at school. The worst thing is that Evilomami, his Maternal Unit, humiliates Julian by insisting he dispose of a "large canister, filled to the brim with humanoid refuse." The Mothership decides to beam Julian aboard and annihilate the planet. Julian stops them, stating, "The Earthlings' brains are limited. . . . They know not what they do!" He decides to continue living with them. This is the first book in the Julian Rodriguez series.

Laugh-Out-Loud Selection: The whole book won't take too long to read. Funny highlights include the fact that Julian attends Aretha Franklin Elementary School. At the end of the book, Julian tells his mother, "You don't know how close you came to total annihilation today," to which his mother replies, "I was just about to say the same thing to you."

Yee, Lisa. *Millicent Min, Girl Genius.* Scholastic, 2003.

Ages 10–12. Millicent is an eleven-year-old girl who has skipped several grades. She makes anagrams out of her Alpha-Bits, "but the vowels keep sinking." She considers herself normal but concedes, "The complex inner workings of my brain probably scare people and repel any potential friends." She does make a new friend in Emily, but Millicent hides her IQ from her. Unfortunately, that plan backfires.

Laugh-Out-Loud Selection: Read the chapter titled "June 9." Millicent discusses her first few days of attending high school, even though she's "a foot shorter and five years younger than [her] peers." She's vilified for being "the one who brings up the curve." She's also horrified when her grandmother Maddie accompanies her to her first-period class. Hearing a disparaging remark, Maddie warns the high school students that she knows kung fu. After Maddie makes several impressive but threatening moves, the kids back away. "When she was done . . . Maddie was still in her age-defying leg-split position. 'Get up,' I hissed. 'Everyone's staring.' 'No can do,' she whispered. 'I appear to be stuck.'"

In addition to the titles listed above, the following chapter book series, which began being published pre-2000 and continued into the following decade, are also highly recommended:

- Captain Underpants series by Dav Pilkey
- Junie B. Jones series by Barbara Park
- A Series of Unfortunate Events by Lemony Snicket
- The Time Warp Trio series by Jon Scieszka

15

POETRY

Agee, Jon. *Orangutan Tongs: Poems to Tangle Your Tongue.* Hyperion, 2009.

Ages 9–12. One highlight from this collection of tongue-twister poems is "Walter and the Waiter." Walter first complains his water is watered down and then that it's too dry. "I like my water wet." The waiter dumps a pitcher of water over Walter's head. The poem "Dodos" shows that dodo birds do little besides dawdle, diddle, "doodle a doodle or two," yodel, and coo.

**Aylesworth, Jim. *The Burger and the Hot Dog.*
Illustrated by Stephen Gammell. Atheneum, 2001.**

Ages 5–9. Puns and wordplay about food are captured in this collection. "Bums" features a group of cookies chasing a bagel. They trip, and "now they're cookie crumbs." Two eggs in "Yack and Yimmy" tell jokes because "they're both so full of yokes." In "How Bleak," sticks of gum look up at the bottom of stools and see the frightening remains of former companions stuck underneath the seats.

Bagert, Brod. *Giant Children.* Illustrated by Tedd Arnold. Dial, 2002.

Ages 5–9. A poem about boogers comes complete with a "WARNING TO ALL CHILDREN: This poem is totally disgusting, and should not, under any circumstances, be recited to a grown-up!" The best combo poems are "Pretty Ribbon," a poem about a brother who wants to use a snake he's found as a ribbon in his sister's hair, and "Jaws," in which the sister retaliates by encouraging a turtle to bite her brother a second time.

Brown, Calef. *Soup for Breakfast.* **Houghton Mifflin, 2008.**

Ages 6–10. A boy dreams of having bear paws instead of hands, young children who grow up to be architects are known as "architots," and a cat turns into a two-dimensional creature when it's hot outside. The kids will love to be grossed out by Grandpa's mustache once they know it's his overly long nose hair. Grandma doesn't care. "She can't hear. Too much ear hair."

DiPucchio, Kelly S. *Sipping Spiders through a Straw:*
Camping Songs for Monsters. **Illustrated by Gris Grimly. Scholastic, 2008.**

Ages 9–12. "Take Me Out to the Graveyard," sung to the tune of "Take Me Out to the Ball Game," makes a fun follow-up activity for a class reading *The Graveyard Book,* by Neil Gaiman (HarperCollins, 2008). "For He's a Stinky Old Fellow" might become a popular party substitute for the song "For He's a Jolly Good Fellow." The other highlight is the ghoulish takeoff of "Do Your Ears Hang Low?" titled "Do Your Guts Hang Low?" "Can you tie them in a knot? / Can you feed them to a crow?"

Florian, Douglas. *Bow Wow Meow Meow:*
It's Rhyming Cats and Dogs. **Harcourt, 2003.**

Ages 5–9. Several breeds of both dogs and cats, including big cats like the black panther and the leopard, are featured. The funniest poems feature a Persian cat who brags about being "purrrsian," a dachshund who is a limousine for fleas, a bloodhound with "scent-sational" senses, and a pointer who always "points at Frigidaires." Florian has several companion books featuring other members of the animal kingdom, including *Mammalabilia: Poems and Paintings* (Harcourt, 2000); *Lizards, Frogs, and Polliwogs: Poems and Paintings* (Harcourt, 2001); and *Omnibeasts: Animal Poems and Paintings* (Harcourt, 2004).

Grandits, John. *Technically, It's Not My Fault:*
Concrete Poems. **Houghton Mifflin, 2004.**

Ages 9–12. This collection of concrete poems includes the visualization of young Robert playing a game of basketball in "The Lay-Up" and another featuring baseball, titled "Robert's Four At-Bats." Robert performs a long series of skateboard tricks in "Skateboard." People yell at him about skateboarding where he shouldn't be. He gives it up. His parents then complain, "You begged for that skateboard, Robert. Now go out and use it!" There is also Robert's vivid image of the toilet in "Sick Day." The highlight is Robert's "The Thank-You Letter," complete with sarcastic footnotes. Grandits delivered another collection of concrete poems with *Blue Lipstick: Concrete Poems* (Clarion, 2007).

Hoberman, Mary Ann. *You Read to Me, I'll Read to You: Very Short Fairy Tales to Read Together.* Illustrated by Michael Emberley. Little, Brown, 2004.

Ages 8–10. Each poem is designed for two voices. In most cases, the adversaries settle their differences and read their own stories to each other. Little Red Riding Hood lets the wolf know that she doesn't believe for even one minute that he is her grandmother. The biggest billy goat learns that the troll needs the money he makes from allowing others to cross the bridge to support his brothers. The troll is sorry he frightened the goats. The princess from "The Princess and the Pea" has quite a dialogue with the pea itself. The funniest image in the book is the wolf from "Little Red Riding Hood" coughing up Grandma, who is still dazed at the end of the poem. This is one of many in the You Read to Me, I'll Read to You series.

Katz, Alan. *Take Me Out of the Bathtub, and Other Silly Dilly Songs.* Illustrated by David Catrow. Margaret K. McElderry, 2001.

Ages 5–12. Katz has created new lyrics to popular songs. "Stinky, Stinky Diaper Change" is set to the tune of "Twinkle, Twinkle, Little Star," and "Give Me a Break," a complaint about overdue library books, is set to the tune of "Home on the Range." Katz has several other books written in a similar format, including *I'm Still Here in the Bathtub: Brand New Silly Dilly Songs* (Margaret K. McElderry, 2003); *On Top of the Potty, and Other Get-Up-and-Go Songs* (Margaret K. McElderry, 2008); and *Smelly Locker: Silly Dilly School Songs* (Margaret K. McElderry, 2008).

Kennedy, X. J. *Exploding Gravy: Poems to Make You Laugh.* Illustrated by Joy Allen. Little, Brown, 2002.

Ages 9–12. The very first poem in the book, "Mother's Nerves," sets the tone. Mother threatens to jump into the stove the next time the screen door slams, and sure enough, "I gave it a bang and in she dove." Another highlight is the limerick ode to reading "Hooked on Books." A man continues to read a book after he hangs his coat on the hook (the man is still wearing the coat).

Lansky, Bruce, ed. *Oh My Darling Porcupine, and Other Silly Sing-Along Songs.* Illustrated by Stephen Carpenter. Meadowbrook, 2006.

Ages 5–12. One of the grosser (but still silly) songs is "The Top of My Hot Dog," set to the tune of "On Top of Old Smoky." A seagull deposits a topping for the narrator's hot dog. Another silly poem is the lengthy "Bring Back My Sister to Me," set to the tune of "My Bonnie." Sister falls down the toilet. She's followed by brother, father, mother, kitty, and dog.

Lewis, J. Patrick. *Once Upon a Tomb: Gravely Humorous Verses.*
Illustrated by Simon Bartram. Candlewick, 2006.

Ages 8–12. Lewis composed twenty-two epitaphs—for an underwear salesman, dairy farmer, fisherman, poet, fortune-teller, food critic, principal, tattoo artist, movie star, bully, soccer player, beautician, weight lifter, cafeteria lady, and more. There's even one for a grave digger, stating that it's a good thing he died, or "He'd have to dig himself a hole."

Prelutsky, Jack. *Awful Ogre's Awful Day.*
Illustrated by Paul O. Zelinsky. Greenwillow, 2001.

Ages 7–11. Awful Ogre boasts that he's "awfulest of all." In "Awful Ogre Pens a Letter," he writes to an ogress and longs for her "craggy gray face." He also calls her "Demure and petite / Just fourteen-foot-four / From your head to your feet." The collection ends with "Awful Ogre's Awful Dream," which finds Awful Ogre dreaming of meandering through a beautiful landscape. "I have never had a nightmare / Nearly half this bad before." The ogre returns in *Awful Ogre Running Wild* (Greenwillow, 2008).

Rex, Adam. *Frankenstein Makes a Sandwich.* **Harcourt, 2006.**

Ages 9–12. The titles of the poems give clues to the zany content of this collection, devoted to movie monsters: "The Phantom of the Opera Can't Get 'It's a Small World' Out of His Head," "The Creature from the Black Lagoon Doesn't Wait an Hour before Swimming," "Bigfoot Can't Believe You Called Him Yeti Just Now," and my favorite, "Count Dracula Doesn't Know He's Been Walking around All Night with Spinach in His Teeth." The companion book is *Frankenstein Takes the Cake* (Harcourt, 2008).

Scieszka, Jon. *Science Verse.* **Illustrated by Lane Smith. Viking, 2004.**

Ages 9–12. A boy is stricken with "a curse of science verse" while listening to his science teacher. He thinks of poetic parodies that deal with different aspects of science. The highlight is the adaption of "Jack Be Nimble." Instead of jumping over a candlestick, Jack jumps over "the combustion reaction of O_2 + heat + fuel to form CO_2 + light + heat + exhaust." This is a companion to Scieszka's nonpoetry book *Math Curse* (Viking, 1995).

Shields, Carol Diggory. *Someone Used My Toothbrush, and Other Bathroom Poems.* **Illustrated by Paul Meisel. Dutton, 2010.**

Ages 5–9. The bathroom is an important room in the house. "Soaked 1" shows what happens when you bathe a dog, and "Soaked 2" warns about the hazards of bathing a cat. A boy has trouble sleeping because of a "Drip." The medicine cabinet contains everything under the sun: "Sprays for noses, feet, and pits / Half-a-dozen cures for zits." The book's title poem tells of a worried boy who believes his sister used his toothbrush "to scrub our pet iguana."

Sierra, Judy. *Monster Goose.* Illustrated by Jack E. Davis. Harcourt, 2001.

Ages 6–12. What if Mother Goose was actually an evil goose who cranked out ghoulish nursery rhymes? Little Miss Muffet becomes "Little Miss Mummy," the old woman who lived in a shoe becomes "There Was an Old Zombie," Little Bo Peep becomes "Werewolf Bo-Creep," and Little Jack Horner becomes "Cannibal Horner," who "Sat in a corner / Eating a people potpie."

Weinstock, Robert. *Can You Dig It? and Other Poems.* Hyperion, 2010.

Ages 6–10. This collection of poems features dinosaurs and aspects of early human life. The highlight is "Coprolite," which tells about LuAnn Abrue, a paleontologist who was famous for "finding fossil poo / Like giant T. rex number two." LuAnn was often heard to say, "You are not only what you eat, / You also are what you excrete."

16

DERIVATIVE LITERATURE—FOLKLORE

"**DERIVATIVE LITERATURE**" refers to modern-day parodies of traditional stories and songs. These are also called fractured fairy tales. The following is a select list of humorous derivative literature published between 2000 and 2010, available in print at the time of this writing, and grouped by the traditional stories they "honor."

Stories Featuring Several Folklore Characters in One Book
See also Mother Goose Nursery Rhymes

Ada, Alma Flor. *Extra! Extra! Fairy-Tale News from Hidden Forest.* Illustrated by Leslie Tryon. Simon and Schuster, 2007. Ages 4–8.

Ada, Alma Flor. *With Love, Little Red Hen.* Illustrated by Leslie Tryon. Atheneum, 2001. Ages 4–8.

Alley, Zoë B. *There's a Wolf at the Door: Five Classic Tales.* Illustrated by R. W. Alley. Roaring Brook, 2008. Ages 5–10.

Burgess, Mark. *Where Teddy Bears Come From.* Illustrated by Russell Ayta. Peachtree, 2008. Ages 4–8.

Catalanotto, Peter. *Ivan the Terrier.* Atheneum, 2007. Ages 3–5.

Child, Lauren. *Who's Afraid of the Big Bad Book?* Hyperion, 2003. Ages 4–9.

Conway, David. *The Great Nursery Rhyme Disaster.* Illustrated by Melanie Williamson. Tiger Tales, 2009. Ages 4–8.

Dealey, Erin. *Goldie Locks Has Chicken Pox*. Illustrated by Hanako Wakiyama. Atheneum, 2002. Ages 4–8.

Grindley, Sally. *Who Is It?* Illustrated by Rosalind Beardshaw. Peachtree, 2000. Ages 3–6.

Hoberman, Mary Ann. *You Read to Me, I'll Read to You: Very Short Fables to Read Together*. Illustrated by Michael Emberley. Little, Brown, 2010. Ages 4–8.

Hoberman, Mary Ann. *You Read to Me, I'll Read to You: Very Short Fairy Tales to Read Together*. Illustrated by Michael Emberley. Little, Brown, 2004. Ages 4–8.

Kloske, Geoffrey. *Once Upon a Time, the End: Asleep in 60 Seconds*. Illustrated by Barry Blitt. Atheneum, 2005. Ages 4–9.

Morgan, Mary. *Dragon Pizzeria*. Knopf, 2008. Ages 4–8.

Palatini, Margie. *Bad Boys*. Illustrated by Henry Cole. HarperCollins, 2003. Ages 4–9.

Palatini, Margie. *Gone with the Wand: A Fairy's Tale*. Illustrated by Brian Ajhar. Orchard, 2009. Ages 5–10.

Ransom, Jeanie Franz. *What Really Happened to Humpty? (From the Files of a Hard-Boiled Detective)*. Illustrated by Stephen Axelsen. Charlesbridge, 2009. Ages 5–10.

Sharratt, Nick. *The Foggy Foggy Forest*. Candlewick, 2008. Ages 3–7.

Sierra, Judy. *Mind Your Manners, B.B. Wolf*. Illustrated by J. Otto Seibold. Knopf, 2007. Ages 4–8.

Stein, David Ezra. *Interrupting Chicken*. Candlewick, 2010. Ages 3–8.

The Boy Who Cried Wolf

Hartman, Bob. *The Wolf Who Cried Boy*. Illustrated by Tim Raglin. Putnam, 2002. Ages 3–8.

Levine, Gail Carson. *Betsy Who Cried Wolf*. Illustrated by Scott Nash. HarperCollins, 2002. Ages 3–8.

Wattenberg, Jane. *Never Cry Woof! A Dog-u-Drama*. Scholastic, 2005. Ages 4–8.

The Bremen Town Musicians

DeFelice, Cynthia. *Old Granny and the Bean Thief*. Illustrated by Cat Bowman Smith. Farrar Straus Giroux, 2003. Ages 5–9.

Huling, Jan. *Ol Bloo's Boogie-Woogie Band and Blues Ensemble*. Illustrated by Henri Sorensen. Peachtree, 2010. Ages 5–8.

O'Malley, Kevin. *Animal Crackers Fly the Coop*. Walker, 2010. Ages 5–9.

Chicken Little/Henny Penny

Dubosarsky, Ursula. *The Terrible Plop*. Illustrated by Andrew Joyner. Farrar Straus Giroux, 2009. Ages 3–6.

Emberley, Rebecca. *Chicken Little*. Illustrated by Ed Emberley. Roaring Brook, 2009. Ages 3–6.

Gorbachev, Valeri. *Dragon Is Coming!* Harcourt, 2009. Ages 4–7.

Graves, Keith. *Chicken Big*. Chronicle, 2010. Ages 4–7.

Palatini, Margie. *Earthquack!* Illustrated by Barry Moser. Simon and Schuster, 2002. Ages 5–8.

Cinderella

Holub, Joan. *Cinderdog and the Wicked Stepcat*. Whitman, 2001. Ages 4–8.

Krensky, Stephen. *The Youngest Fairy Godmother Ever*. Illustrated by Diana Cain Bluthenthal. Simon and Schuster, 2000. Ages 5–8.

Lowell, Susan. *Cindy Ellen: A Wild Western Cinderella*. Illustrated by Jane Manning. HarperCollins, 2000. Ages 5–8.

San Souci, Robert. *Cinderella Skeleton*. Illustrated by David Catrow. Silver Whistle, 2000. Ages 6–8.

Sierra, Judy. *The Gift of the Crocodile: A Cinderella Story*. Illustrated by Reynold Ruffins. Simon and Schuster, 2000. Ages 6–8.

The Fox and the Grapes

Palatini, Margie. *Lousy Rotten Stinkin' Grapes*. Illustrated by Barry Moser. Simon and Schuster, 2009. Ages 4–8.

The Frog Prince

Allchin, Rosalind. *The Frog Princess*. Kids Can, 2001. Ages 5–9.

Bardhan-Quallen, Sudipta. *The Hog Prince*. Illustrated by Jason Wolff. Dutton, 2009. Ages 4–8.

Hopkins, Jackie Mims. *The Horned Toad Prince*. Illustrated by Michael Austin. Peachtree, 2000. Ages 5–8.

Novak, Matt. *My Froggy Valentine*. Roaring Brook, 2008. Ages 4–8.

Ormerod, Jan. *The Frog Princess*. Illustrated by Emma Damon. Hodder, 2004. Ages 4–8.

The Gingerbread Man

Ernst, Lisa Campbell. *The Gingerbread Girl.* Dutton, 2006. Ages 3–8.

Palatini, Margie. *Bad Boys Get Cookie!* Illustrated by Henry Cole. HarperCollins, 2006. Ages 4–8.

Shulman, Janet. *The Matzo Ball Boy.* Illustrated by Rosanne Litzinger. Dutton, 2005. Ages 5–8.

Squires, Janet. *The Gingerbread Cowboy.* Illustrated by Holly Berry. HarperCollins, 2006. Ages 4–8.

Goldilocks and the Three Bears

Catalano, Dominic. *Santa and the Three Bears.* Boyds Mills, 2000. Ages 4–8.

Duval, Kathy. *The Three Bears' Christmas.* Illustrated by Paul Meisel. Holiday House, 2005. Ages 4–8.

Duval, Kathy. *The Three Bears' Halloween.* Illustrated by Paul Meisel. Holiday House, 2007. Ages 4–8.

Elya, Susan Middleton. *Rubia and the Three Osos.* Illustrated by Melissa Sweet. Hyperion, 2010. Ages 5–8.

Ernst, Lisa Campbell. *Goldilocks Returns.* Simon and Schuster, 2000. Ages 4–8.

Fearnley, Jan. *Mr. Wolf and the Three Bears.* Harcourt, 2002. Ages 3–8.

Lester, Helen. *Tackylocks and the Three Bears.* Illustrated by Lynn Munsinger. Houghton Mifflin, 2002. Ages 3–8.

Lowell, Susan. *Dusty Locks and the Three Bears.* Holt, 2001. Ages 4–9.

Stanley, Diane. *Goldie and the Three Bears.* HarperCollins, 2003. Ages 5–8.

Hansel and Gretel

Gordon, David. *Hansel and Diesel.* HarperCollins, 2006. Ages 4–7.

Jack and the Beanstalk

Artell, Mike. *Jacques and de Beanstalk.* Illustrated by Jim Harris. Dial, 2010. Ages 5–9.

Birdseye, Tom. *Look Out, Jack! The Giant Is Back!* Illustrated by Will Hillenbrand. Holiday House, 2001. Ages 4–8.

Ketteman, Helen. *Waynetta and the Cornstalk: A Texas Fairy Tale.* Illustrated by Diane Greenseid. Albert Whitman, 2007. Ages 4–8.

Osborne, Mary Pope. *Kate and the Beanstalk.* Illustrated by Giselle Potter. Atheneum, 2000. Ages 5–10.

Stanley, Diane. *The Giant and the Beanstalk.* HarperCollins, 2004. Ages 4–9.

The Little Red Hen
Fields, Terri. *Burro's Tortillas*. Illustrated by Sherry Rogers. Sylvan Dell, 2007. Ages 4–8.

Fleming, Candace. *Gator Gumbo: A Spicy-Hot Tale*. Illustrated by Sally Anne Lambert. Farrar Straus Giroux, 2004. Ages 4–9.

Ketteman, Helen. *Armadilly Chili*. Illustrated by Will Terry. Albert Whitman, 2004. Ages 5–9.

Paul, Ann Whitford. *Mañana Iguana*. Illustrated by Ethan Long. Holiday House, 2004. Ages 5–9.

Little Red Riding Hood
Artell, Mike. *Petite Rouge: A Cajun Red Riding Hood*. Illustrated by Jim Harris. Dial, 2001. Ages 5–10.

Daly, Niki. *Pretty Salma: A Little Red Riding Hood Story from Africa*. Clarion, 2007. Ages 5–9.

Forward, Toby. *The Wolf's Story: What Really Happened to Little Red Riding Hood*. Illustrated by Izhar Cohen. Candlewick, 2005. Ages 5–10.

Levine, Gail Carson. *Betsy Red Hoodie*. Illustrated by Scott Nash. HarperCollins, 2010. Ages 5–8.

Paul, Ann Whitford. *Tortuga in Trouble*. Illustrated by Ethan Long. Holiday House, 2009. Ages 5–9.

Roberts, Lynn. *Little Red: A Fizzingly Good Yarn*. Illustrated by David Roberts. Abrams, 2005. Ages 5–8.

Yep, Laurence. *Auntie Tiger*. Illustrated by Insu Lee. HarperCollins, 2008. Ages 5–9.

Mother Goose Nursery Rhymes
Baker, Keith. *Hickory Dickory Dock*. Harcourt, 2007. Ages 3–6.

Bar-el, Dan. *Things Are Looking Grimm, Jill*. Orca, 2006. Ages 4–7.

Dealey, Erin. *Little Bo Peep Can't Get to Sleep*. Illustrated by Hanako Wakiyama. Atheneum, 2005. Ages 4–8.

Harris, Trudy. *The Clock Struck One: A Time-Telling Tale*. Illustrated by Carrie Hartman. Millbrook, 2009. Ages 4–8.

Hoberman, Mary Ann. *You Read to Me, I'll Read to You: Very Short Mother Goose Tales to Read Together*. Illustrated by Michael Emberley. Little, Brown, 2005. Ages 4–8.

Horowitz, Dave. *Humpty Dumpty Climbs Again*. Putnam, 2008. Ages 4–8.

Kirk, Daniel. *Jack and Jill.* Putnam, 2003. Ages 3–8.

Robinson, Hilary. *Over the Moon!* Illustrated by Jane Abbott. Crabtree, 2010. Ages 3–8.

Seibold, J. Otto. *Other Goose: Re-Nurseried, Re-Rhymed, Re-Mothered, and Re-Goosed.* Chronicle, 2010. Ages 5–10.

Sierra, Judy. *Monster Goose.* Illustrated by Jack E. Davis. Harcourt, 2001. Ages 5–10.

Stevens, Janet, and Susan Stevens Crummel. *And the Dish Ran Away with the Spoon.* Harcourt, 2001. Ages 5–9.

The Old Woman and Her Pig

Jackson, Alison. *Desert Rose and Her Highfalutin Hog.* Illustrated by Keith Graves. Walker, 2009. Ages 5–9.

The Princess and the Pea

Auch, Mary Jane. *The Princess and the Pizza.* Illustrated by Herm Auch. Holiday House, 2002. Ages 5–9.

Edwards, Pamela Duncan. *Princess Pigtoria and the Pea.* Illustrated by Henry Cole. Orchard, 2010. Ages 4–8.

Grey, Mini. *The Very Smart Pea and the Princess-to-Be.* Knopf, 2003. Ages 4–9.

Perlman, Janet. *The Penguin and the Pea.* Kids Can, 2004. Ages 4–8.

Rapunzel

Roberts, Lynn. *Rapunzel: A Groovy Fairy Tale.* Illustrated by David Roberts. Abrams, 2003. Ages 4–9.

Wilcox, Leah. *Falling for Rapunzel.* Illustrated by Lydia Monks. Putnam, 2003. Ages 4–9.

Sleeping Beauty

Hale, Bruce. *Snoring Beauty.* Illustrated by Howard Fine. Harcourt, 2008. Ages 4–9.

Osborne, Will, and Mary Pope Osborne. *Sleeping Bobby.* Illustrated by Giselle Potter. Atheneum, 2005. Ages 4–10.

Wilcox, Leah. *Waking Beauty.* Illustrated by Lydia Monks. Putnam, 2008. Ages 4–9.

The Three Billy Goats Gruff

Hassett, John, and Ann Hassett. *The Three Silly Girls Grubb.* Houghton Mifflin, 2002. Ages 4–8.

Hopkins, Jackie. *The Three Armadillies Tuff.* Illustrated by S. G. Brooks. Peachtree, 2002. Ages 4–9.

Kimmel, Eric. *The Three Cabritos*. Illustrated by Stephen Gilpin. Marshall
   Cavendish, 2007. Ages 4–9.
Palatini, Margie. *The Three Silly Billies*. Illustrated by Barry Moser. Simon and
   Schuster, 2005. Ages 4–9.

The Three Little Pigs

Artell, Mike. *Three Little Cajun Pigs*. Illustrated by Jim Harris. Dial, 2003. Ages
   4–8.
Brett, Jan. *The 3 Little Dassies*. Putnam, 2010. Ages 4–8.
Geist, Ken. *The Three Little Fish and the Big Bad Shark*. Illustrated by Julia
   Gorton. Scholastic, 2007. Ages 3–8.
Guarnaccia, Steven. *The Three Little Pigs: An Architectural Tale*. Abrams, 2010.
   Ages 4–9.
Ketteman, Helen. *The Three Little Gators*. Illustrated by Will Terry. Albert
   Whitman, 2009. Ages 3–8.
Kimmel, Eric A. *The Three Little Tamales*. Illustrated by Valeria Docampo.
   Marshall Cavendish, 2009. Ages 4–7.
Pichon, Liz. *The Three Horrid Little Pigs*. Tiger Tales, 2008. Ages 3–8.
Seabrooke, Brenda. *Wolf Pie*. Illustrated by Liz Callen. Clarion, 2010. Ages 6–8.
Sierra, Judy. *Tell the Truth, B.B. Wolf*. Illustrated by J. Otto Seibold. Knopf, 2010.
   Ages 4–8.
Wiesner, David. *The Three Pigs*. Clarion, 2001. Ages 4–9.

The Three Peaches

Bar-el, Dan. *Such a Prince*. Illustrated by John Manders. Clarion, 2007. Ages 7–11.

The Tortoise and the Hare

Cuyler, Margery. *Road Signs: A Harey Race with a Tortoise*. Illustrated by Steve
   Haskamp. Winslow, 2000. Ages 3–7.
Downard, Barry. *The Race of the Century*. Simon and Schuster, 2008. Ages 4–8.
Repchuk, Caroline. *The Race*. Illustrated by Alison Jay. Chronicle, 2002. Ages 4–8.

17

DERIVATIVE LITERATURE—SONGS

The Eensy Weensy Spider

Cummings, Troy. *The Eensy Weensy Spider Freaks Out! (Big Time).* Random House, 2010. Ages 3–7.

If You're Happy and You Know It

Emberley, Rebecca. *If You're a Monster and You Know It.* Illustrated by Ed Emberley. Orchard, 2010. Ages 3–8.

Little Bunny Foo Foo

Johnson, Paul Brett. *Little Bunny Foo Foo.* Scholastic, 2004. Ages 3–8.

Old MacDonald Had a Farm

Carter, Don. *Old MacDonald Drives a Tractor.* Roaring Brook, 2007. Ages 3–7.
Tobin, Jim. *Sue MacDonald Had a Book.* Illustrated by Dave Coverly. Holt, 2009. Ages 4–7.

On Top of Old Smoky

Johnson, Paul Brett. *On Top of Spaghetti.* Scholastic, 2006. Ages 3–8.

She'll Be Coming 'Round the Mountain

Reid, Rob. *Comin' Down to Storytime.* Illustrated by Nadine Bernard Westcott. Upstart, 2009. Ages 3–7.

There Was an Old Lady Who Swallowed a Fly

Bowen, Anne. *I Know an Old Teacher.* Illustrated by Stephen Gammell.
Carolrhoda, 2008. Ages 5–9.

Colandro, Lucille. *There Was an Old Lady Who Swallowed a Bat.* Illustrated by
Jared Lee. Scholastic, 2002. Ages 4–8.

Colandro, Lucille. *There Was an Old Lady Who Swallowed a Bell.* Illustrated by
Jared Lee. Scholastic, 2006. Ages 4–8.

Colandro, Lucille. *There Was an Old Lady Who Swallowed a Chick.* Illustrated by
Jared Lee. Scholastic, 2009. Ages 4–8.

Colandro, Lucille. *There Was an Old Lady Who Swallowed a Shell.* Illustrated by
Jared Lee. Scholastic, 2006. Ages 4–8.

Colandro, Lucille. *There Was an Old Lady Who Swallowed Some Leaves.*
Illustrated by Jared Lee. Scholastic, 2010. Ages 4–8.

Colandro, Lucille. *There Was an Old Lady Who Swallowed Some Snow.* Illustrated
by Jared Lee. Scholastic, 2003. Ages 4–8.

Emberley, Rebecca, Adrian Emberley, and Ed Emberley. *There Was an Old
Monster.* Orchard, 2009. Ages 4–8.

Garriel, Barbara S. *I Know a Shy Fellow Who Swallowed a Cello.* Illustrated by
John O'Brien. Boyds Mills, 2004. Ages 4–8.

Ward, Jennifer. *There Was a Coyote Who Swallowed a Flea.* Illustrated by Steve
Gray. Rising Moon, 2007. Ages 4–8.

Ward, Jennifer. *There Was an Old Monkey Who Swallowed a Frog.* Illustrated by
Steve Gray. Marshall Cavendish, 2010. Ages 4–8.

The Wheels on the Bus

Dale, Penny. *The Boy on the Bus.* Candlewick, 2007. Ages 3–7.

Hort, Lenny. *The Seals on the Bus.* Illustrated by G. Brian Karas. Holt, 2000.
Ages 3–7.

Mills, Elizabeth J. *The Spooky Wheels on the Bus.* Illustrated by Ben Mantle.
Scholastic, 2010. Ages 4–8.

Zane, Alexander. *The Wheels on the Race Car.* Illustrated by James Warhola.
Scholastic, 2005. Ages 4–8.

THE COVETED ROBBIE AWARDS

THERE ARE already many, many children's book awards out there (well over three hundred). There are even two awards that deal specifically with children's humor—the Sid Fleischman Award and the Roald Dahl Funny Prize. But neither has the distinction associated with the Coveted (the term *coveted* was added last year) Robbie Awards, in which a distinguished panel of experts (me) selects the funniest children's picture book and chapter book of the year (and sometimes Ɨ we inform the winners).

2000
Picture Book: *Olivia* by Ian Falconer
Chapter Book: *No More Dead Dogs* by Gordon Korman
Chapter Book Honor: *A Year Down Yonder* by Richard Peck

2001
Picture Book: *Widget* by Lyn Rossiter McFarland
Chapter Book: *The Amazing Maurice and His Educated Rodents* by Terry Pratchett

2002
Picture Book: *I Stink!* by Kate McMullan
Chapter Book: *Jake Drake, Class Clown* by Andrew Clements

2003

Picture Book: *Don't Let the Pigeon Drive the Bus!* by Mo Willems
Picture Book Honor: *Bad Boys* by Margie Palatini
Picture Book Honor: *Arnie the Doughnut* by Laurie Keller
Chapter Book: *Millicent Min, Girl Genius* by Lisa Yee
Chapter Book Honor: *How Angel Peterson Got His Name* by Gary Paulsen

2004

Picture Book: *Knuffle Bunny* by Mo Willems
Picture Book Honor: *The Best Pet of All* by David LaRochelle
Chapter Book: *The Pepins and Their Problems* by Polly Horvath

2005

Picture Book: *Punk Farm* by Jarrett Krosoczka
Picture Book Honor: *Bad Kitty* by Nick Bruel
Chapter Book: *Mr. Chickee's Funny Money* by Christopher Paul Curtis

2006

Picture Book: *Dooby Dooby Moo* by Doreen Cronin
Picture Book Honor: *Chickens to the Rescue* by John Himmelman
Chapter Book: *Ivy and Bean and the Ghost That Had to Go* by Annie Barrows

2007

Picture Book: *Pssst!* by Adam Rex
Chapter Book: *Diary of a Wimpy Kid* by Jeff Kinney

2008

Picture Book: *The Scrambled States of America* by Laurie Keller
Chapter Book: *The Willoughbys* by Lois Lowry

2009

Picture Book: *Rhyming Dust Bunnies* by Jan Thomas
Chapter Book: *Jasper Dash and the Flame-Pits of Delaware* by M. T. Anderson

2010

Picture Book: *Rescue Bunnies* by Doreen Cronin
Chapter Book: *Attack of the Fluffy Bunnies* by Andrea Beaty
Chapter Book Honor: *The Adventures of Nanny Piggins* by R. A. Spratt

INDEX

Page numbers in bold indicate an annotation.

You may also be interested in

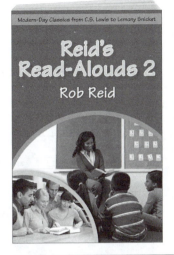

REID'S READ-ALOUDS 2
Modern-Day Classics from
C. S. Lewis to Lemony Snicket
Rob Reid

Need a one-stop resource for jumpstarting sleepy library visitors? Ready to add punch to classroom discussions? In this companion to his best-selling book *Reid's Read-Alouds*, children's lit guru Rob Reid dips back into the classics to highlight outstanding titles published between 1950 and 1999 that continue to connect with kids and teens today.

ISBN: 978-0-8389-1072-6
160 PAGES / 6" × 9"

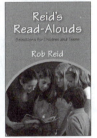

REID'S READ-ALOUDS
Selections for Children and Teens
ISBN: 978-0-8389-0980-5

MORE FAMILY STORYTIMES
24 Creative Programs for All Ages
ISBN: 978-0-8389-0973-7

SOMETHING MUSICAL HAPPENED AT THE LIBRARY Adding Song and Dance to Children's Story Programs
ISBN: 978-0-8389-0942-3

CHILDREN'S JUKEBOX, 2E The Select Subject Guide to Children's Musical Recordings
ISBN: 978-0-8389-0940-9

SOMETHING FUNNY HAPPENED AT THE LIBRARY
ISBN: 978-0-8389-0836-5

FAMILY STORYTIME
24 Creative Programs for All Ages
ISBN: 978-0-8389-0751-1